I'm No Superman:
Holy Spirit Ministry
For The Rest Of Us

MIKE TURRIGIANO

WITH LUKE GERATY

DEDICATION

To all those many followers of Jesus who dream of being used by God to help advance his kingdom but disqualify themselves because they consider themselves too unqualified and ordinary. This book is for you...

THE MAIN AND PLAIN

Coaching & Guidance for Pastors
We're certified coaches who can help pastors and leaders overcome specific obstacles or provide guidance either in person or over the phone/Skype.

Seminars & Retreats
For over 40 years we have helped churches through the U.S. and Europe engage with the activity of the Holy Spirit, develop an inner life with God, and leadership development.

Guest Preaching
Having pastored for almost 40 years, we would love to serve your church by preaching about a variety of topics.

Blog & Webcasts
We're able to connect with and reach lots of people through our regular musing on life and faith in Jesus through these valuable virtual channels.

For more info visit www.themainandplain.com

CONTENTS

ACKNOWLEDGMENTS

Someone very wise once wrote, "There is nothing new under the sun." Nothing in this book is original. I'm only passing on to you what's been passed on to me by gifted teachers and mentors who took me under their wings and apprenticed me in the things of the Spirit. All I've done is manage to put them to use over a lifetime of pastoral ministry.

So I want to thank some of those people who helped open my eyes and turn me into the Spirit-adventurer I am today. First, I have to thank John Wimber for being the "naturally supernatural" model that set me free, unlocking Holy Spirit ministry for me while allowing me to remain grounded and real. Lonnie Frisbee-- for lighting the fuse that launched me into Holy Spirit ministry orbit.
Lance Pittluck-- for teaching me how to be a spiritual leader. I want to thank the congregations I had the privilege of serving that became the Spirit-laboratories where I learned to put all these things into practice.

Thank you, Luke Geraty for being willing to partner with me and adding polish to this project. I want to give a very special thanks to Todd Kennedy, my editor, for his scholarly theological insights and corrections that will hopefully keep me from being labeled a heretic.

I also want to thank my son Matthew for his design work and being willing to do the tedious work of formatting and inputting the book into the publisher's template. And of course, to my wife Char, thank you for always being there cheering me on.

MIKE'S INTRODUCTION

I'm a New Yorker, born and raised. In the neighborhood I grew up in we had a saying that stuck with me: "Don't believe anything you hear and only half of what you see!" Even after becoming a Jesus follower I had a hard time swallowing much of the charismatic sensationalism and hoopla. So, the fact that today I have wholeheartedly embraced the supernatural and become a proponent of the use of spiritual gifts is in itself a minor miracle! What turned it around for me?

Getting in on the action
Moving from being a skeptic to a practitioner required a shift in my worldview that involved four things: a genuine experience, a credible model, a reasonable explanation, and practice, practice, practice. My hope is that if you find yourself in a place of skepticism this book will help put you on a similar path.

I'm not a theologian. I'm a practitioner and a pragmatist. I've focused most of my nearly five decades of ministry as a church planter and pastor on making life with God as simple and livable as possible. At the risk of making God's mysterious ways too simple, I want to shed light on an area of ministry that a large portion of the Church has relegated to the domain of spiritual superstars and celebrities. This is an unfortunate development that has turned a large portion of the Body of Christ into spectators that sit on the sidelines admiring these spiritual superstars who are having all the fun doing the stuff Jesus did.

The rest of us
Is this what Jesus had in mind when he chose the people he would entrust his ministry to? The people Jesus chose were not the most likely candidates for such a charge. None of them were trained religious professionals. They were mostly ordinary folk--like the rest of us. But they experienced the kingdom of God, and it changed them. In addition, there was the convincing effect that the model of Jesus' compelling life had on them. And on top of that he gave them an explanation of this life that so awakened and captured their imaginations that it turned ordinary men and women into world changers.

I use the phrase "Holy Spirit ministry" as shorthand for all the things that Jesus and his early followers did as they ministered here on earth as reported in the gospels and the Book of Acts. Matthew 4 gives a representative summary:

23 Jesus traveled throughout the region of Galilee, teaching in the synagogues and announcing the Good News about the Kingdom. And he healed every kind of disease and illness. 24 News about him spread as far as Syria, and people soon began bringing to him all who were sick. And whatever their sickness or disease, or if they were demon possessed or epileptic or paralyzed—he healed them all.25 Large crowds followed him wherever he went—people from Galilee, the Ten Towns, Jerusalem, from all over Judea, and from east of the Jordan River. (Matthew 4:23-25)

This is what in the Vineyard we call, "doing the stuff". I believe this sort of Holy Spirit ministry is within the realm of possibility, to one degree or another, for every follower of Christ. Armed with a healthy relationship with Christ and some equipping and coaching, we can learn--with practice-- how to pay attention to the Spirit's promptings (as Jesus did) and utilize the spiritual tools that he makes available to us so that we can join him and the Father in their kingdom work.

In the chapters that follow, I'll offer some perspectives and tips that have helped me in the practice of Holy Spirit ministry in everyday life. I'll cover things like being filled with the Spirit, discerning the Spirit's voice, discovering and exercising spiritual gifts, partnering with the in-the-moment ministry of the Spirit, and other matters involved in everyday life with God's Spirit.

This book isn't for superheroes. It's for the rest of us. It's my attempt to offer help to anyone who wants to get in on the action but lacks instruction or is frustrated for some reason. My hope is that you'll gain a practical, user-friendly grasp of the work of God's kingdom and doing the stuff Jesus did that will lead you to new possibilities-- turning your ordinary, everyday life into a God-adventure. My hope is that it will lead you to a constructive, joyful and fruitful relationship with the Spirit.

I'm coming at the subject of what a life engaged with the Holy Spirit looks like in ordinary, everyday life as one who has learned more practical theology by participating and serving in the community of Christ than in a classroom. In the past whenever I thought I had the Holy Spirit figured out and created a nice neat box to fit him in I found I've always found I needed a bigger box. This book is my attempt to tackle some rather complex and puzzling topics for sure, such as the Trinity and the baptism in the Holy Spirit. So please keep in mind as you read that I write as a witness not as a scholar.

LUKE'S INTRODUCTION

I've known *of* Mike Turrigiano for a long time. Mike's been around the Vineyard since the beginning, which you can read about in his book *How I Got There*, and his legend lives in our movement's folklore.

About five years ago I had the pleasure of getting to actually spend time with Mike and a friendship quickly developed out of that first meeting. I'll never forget that first night we hung out late into the early morning as he shared stories about what it was like to be around John Wimber, to pastor a church in New York, and to carry out ministry in the power of the Holy Spirit that was "naturally supernatural." To put it bluntly, I've learned a *lot* from Mike. Mike and I work well together because we have similar interests, similar ways of doing things, and a similar shared theological commitment – the theology of the kingdom of God.

This book is essentially a "practical theology" of "doing the stuff" in relation to "Holy Spirit ministry." In other words, Mike has written an accessible and easy to understand book that will help you and other readers to better learn the language of the Holy Spirit and to know how to respond to what the Spirit is doing around you. This is the book I will give to people in my church who want to know how to pray for people, how to hear from God, and how to see miraculous things happen without all of the weird stuff that sometimes accompanies "charismatics." Full disclosure: I'm a charismatic.

My spiritual journey includes a long stint studying and earning a few degrees in theology. I believe theology is *extremely* important and that part of loving God, as defined by Jesus, is to be done with our mind (Matt. 22:37). Good theology enhances and enriches Christian discipleship and bad theology has a tendency of hurting people. I make no apologies for being a theologian and encouraging everyone else to think theologically. But I'm also a *pastor* and believe that theology should serve the Church and strengthen followers of Jesus in their participation in kingdom ministry. What excites me about Mike's work is that he offers an extremely practical and authentic window into his "naturally supernatural" walk with the Spirit in a way that will *encourage* and *challenge* you to "get in the game." But it's not only practical, *it's faithful to Scripture!* It's a "best of both worlds" type of offering that maintains the "radical middle" that the Vineyard is known for.

Mike also graciously allowed me to write a chapter on the Holy Spirit that will hopefully encourage you to think beyond where your previous perspective on the Spirit ends (chapter fifteen).

Chapter "Reflection and Action" discussion questions

At the end of each chapter, Mike and I have put together a number of questions for you to use in order to further discuss the topics and put what you learn into action in your everyday lives. These questions are open-ended, and our intention is for them to encourage your group to "go deeper" as they explain their thoughts and opinions. Plus, we hope they are fun too! These questions would be great for a small group or for you to work through with some friends you may think could benefit from the ideas in this book.

PROLOGUE

Do you actually know what you're asking when you pray, *"Come Holy Spirit"?* Do you understand just how risky it is?

It seems like a safe enough prayer. After all, it's spoken in lots of churches these days. But do we really know what we're getting ourselves into when we pray it sincerely? Do we realize we're plunging into a mystery, letting go like trapeze artists from the bar, flying into God's hands in an unfolding moment of trust? *"Come Holy Spirit"* is an invitation to God to have his way with us-- giving him permission do whatever he wants with our lives, any way he wants to do it...

The first person I ever heard pray, "Come Holy Spirit" was Lonnie Frisbee. Lonnie's sort of a legend. He was one of a kind. A hippie mystic birthed out of the Jesus People Movement, Lonnie was traveling with John Wimber, the founder of the Vineyard movement, at the time I met him in 1981. You might say Lonnie-- in the mold of an Old Testament prophet, complete with piercing eyes, shoulder length hair and full beard-- was an *incendiary*. He would call down the power of God, setting churches aflame with the Spirit. The unique thing about Lonnie's ministry was that the fire would remain burning after he left. The Spirit's empowering work continued on without him, like radioactive fallout in the aftermath of a nuclear blast.

I remember the night Lonnie visited our little church in Brooklyn and caused a holy ruckus... After giving his testimony, he had us fold-up our chairs and stand in the middle of the room. Nobody knew quite what to expect next...

Then Lonnie shouted, *"You've been ignoring the Holy Spirit, and it's offended him. Repent! He wants his church back!"* He followed with that prayer, "Come Holy Spirit!" Then silence. The air in our small chapel grew eerily still. There was a weight to it like in a gathering storm. Then suddenly, like a bomb going off, all heaven broke loose, and we were introduced to a side of the Holy Spirit we'd never known: His wild, untamed side.

An irresistible force filled the room. People started wailing and dropping to the floor under the power of the Spirit. It was frightfully wonderful! We were suddenly in the disquieting presence of the all-powerful Beyond... beyond explanation and control. I imagine this is what the gospel writers were referring to when they reported that after witnessing of one of Jesus's miracles, his disciples were left befuddled, awestruck and frightened. Like Peter after the miraculous catch of fish, God's holiness made me painfully aware of my sinfulness. And yet, at the very same time, it seemed I was surrounded by an ocean of love. One moment I was sobbing, the next laughing…

When I think back to that evening and Lonnie's prayer, something the author and poet Annie Dillard wrote captures the moment well:

… Does anyone have the foggiest idea what sort of power we so blithely invoke? Or, as I suspect, does no one believe a word of it? The churches are children playing on the floor with their chemistry sets, mixing up a batch of TNT to kill a Sunday morning. It is madness to wear ladies straw hats and velvet hats to church; we should all be wearing crash helmets. Ushers should issue life preservers and signal flares; they should lash us to our pews. For the sleeping god may wake someday and take offense, or the waking god may draw us out to where we can never return. (from Teaching A Stone To Talk)

We were never the same after that night. We were "drawn out to where we could never return." I was ruined for the presence of God. Life and ministry would never return to business as usual. Nothing could trump God's presence. I understood in a new way what the psalmist meant when he sang:

As the deer pants for streams of water,
*   so my soul pants for you, my God.*
My soul thirsts for God, for the living God.
*   When can I go and meet with God?*

Now all this is good and right, but if we're not careful our flawed sinful natures can lead us to cross a line and take "Come Holy Spirit" for granted. As Eugene Peterson observed, *"We get bossy and begin speaking and acting for God; we start trying to control God and along the way we take over God's work for him and take charge of making sure things go right. We get a false sense of self-importance, because we've spent so much time around God."*

There's always a temptation to try to manage the Spirit and make things happen—to substitute our own agendas, ego-needs, convenience and comfort for intimacy, worship, and surrender. If we're not careful, "Come Holy Spirit" can become a way of ordering God around rather than an act of self-surrender.

The truth is we're never in the right position when we try to control God.

He's not a God to be tamed or managed. God controls us. That's the essence of "Come Holy Spirit". We need to cultivate the freedom of childlike surrender and trust. Letting go of our need or desire to be in control gives us access to a life that exceeds our capacity to dictate or manage. It allows us to live on the edge of mystery, up on the trapeze, open to God's Spirit flowing around and through us-- a life attentive to God rather than to our self-importance. Worship uninhibited by our ego.

"Come Holy Spirit" isn't a religious slogan. It's an invitation to a person by whom we're led and cared for, a person who puts electricity in our faith and makes our worship an acrobatic letting go landing us smack dab in God's loving arms.

So a warning: Be careful when you pray, "Come Holy Spirit". It's a prayer that is dangerous to egos and self-interests. It challenges us to trust God and venture out beyond ourselves and our ability to control in order to take risks for the sake of Christ and others.

Walter Brueggemann put it this way, *"Taken most simply, Holy Spirit refers to the intruding, invasive, energizing power from God that comes like the wind to blow us beyond ourselves, to take actions, to dare dreams, to run risks that in our accustomed powerlessness are well beyond us... The wind of God will blow us to freedom and courage in spite of our tired fearfulness..."*

I don't know about you, but I want in on God's action that turns life into that trapeze act of trust, launching me out and beyond myself, and makes ordinary, everyday existence a Spirit-led adventure. I hope the following offerings help you along the way... "Come Holy Spirit".

1 WHO GETS TO PLAY, REALLY?

Who gets to do the stuff we see Jesus and his followers doing in the Bible? As a result of the celebrity-driven culture that's made its way into the Church, a good many Christians have resigned themselves to the notion that partnering with the Holy Spirit in signs and wonders is out of their league; they're happy to leave it to the anointed and gifted superstars featured at conferences who write the books and post the videos. But if I get the gist of Jesus' Upper Room Discourse (John 14-16), I have to believe that Holy Spirit ministry is meant to be livable and doable for regular, everyday believers, too. Jesus said, *"The truth is, anyone who believes in me will do the same works I have done and even greater works, because I am going to be with the Father." (John 14:12)*

Because every follower of Jesus has the Holy Spirit, I believe that *"everybody can get to play"*-- not necessarily on the big stage but in smaller, less spectacular ways in the course of everyday living. The average recreational basketball lover will never play like LeBron James, but he/she can still enjoy playing the game at a competent level. So it is with the average Christian when it comes to engaging in Holy Spirit ministry. We can all play and enjoy the satisfaction of being used by God, even in extraordinary ways on occasion.

It comes down to being open and alert to God in the little things of life that go on around us all the time—from the ordinary and easily overlooked, to the hidden and the unexpected. Engaging in Holy Spirit ministry begins with learning to be attentive and following the Spirit's lead in the course of the unspectacular everyday where most of us live most of our lives, most of the time.

Because these promptings occur in the midst of the ordinary and the humdrum they can easily go unnoticed.

1

The Holy Spirit can lead us while we're discharging our everyday chores and responsibilities, things we don't necessarily want to do but have to get done nevertheless, things we do while on "autopilot"-- not paying attention because they're routine. The Holy Spirit may be at work as we're on our morning commutes, fixing flat tires, changing diapers, handing in term papers, doing the laundry, standing in lines at the store, making our daily visits to the coffee shop, and engaging in casual conversations.

It's hard to believe that these errands, appointments, happenings, and interactions are the raw material God works with in order to reveal himself and move us to action for his kingdom's sake, but they are. And if you don't know what you're looking for, or if you're not paying attention, they're easy to miss or to dismiss. A glance, a nudge, a sense, a` passing thought, a look on someone's face, something said in a casual conversation: they can all be the Spirit inviting you to join God as he works in the lives of people you come in contact with in the course of your everyday life.

My wife Char was in line at our local pharmacy not too long ago when she noticed the clerk wincing in pain as he worked behind the checkout counter. She sensed God's Spirit prompting her to pray for him right there and then. Despite the awkwardness and risk, when it was her turn to step up to the counter, she asked the clerk if he was okay. He told her that his back had been giving him trouble all day. With a line of impatient customers behind her, Char asked him if she could pray for him, and he said yes! She said a quick healing prayer in the name of Jesus, he thanked her, and she left. A couple of days later Char visited the pharmacy again; when she walked in, the clerk saw her and exclaimed in a loud enough voice for all to hear, "There's my girl! My back has been fine ever since you prayed for me!" All Char did was pay attention and care enough to take a risk, and God showed up and did something wonderful in the ordinary...

Eugene Peterson wrote, *"Spiritual maturity is largely growth in seeing."* That "seeing" includes noticing and responding to what God is doing in the everyday and ordinary. God works in the routine things, so it behooves us to learn how to pay attention. Nobody was better at this than Jesus...

2

In the moment ministry

I find it noteworthy that so much of Jesus' ministry appeared to be unscripted and impromptu, taking place in the marketplace of ordinary life. Conversations, social events, even interruptions, turned out to be occasions for in-breakings of the kingdom. The healing of the paralytic who was lowered by friends through the roof (Luke 5:17-26), the healing of the woman who crept up behind him in a crowd and touched his robe (Luke 8:42b-48), the casual conversation with the woman at the well as he waited for his disciples to return with lunch (John 4:4-26) are just a few examples of how, being in tune with the Spirit, Jesus "saw" what the Father was doing in the hidden, little, ordinary, or unexpected and joined in to produce miraculous results.

Jesus was able to recognize his Father's voice apart from all the other voices that were clamoring for his attention. He was able to slow down and tune out all the distractions, quiet himself in order to pay attention and receive *inward revelation* - "seeing" and "hearing" words of knowledge, prophecy, and wisdom from his Father through the Spirit. His childlike trust and expectant faith allowed him to react spontaneously in the moment, go with the flow of the Spirit, take risks and obey, speak the Father's words and do the Father's works.

In my opinion, these attributes of Jesus' ministry do not come by way of superior knowledge or exceptional anointing and gifting. These capacities aren't just for the elite: it's possible for every disciple to operate like this. This alert responsiveness is the fruit of a love relationship that we're all invited into and capable of developing. Jesus called it *abiding* in him.

My big discovery

I've made an important discovery about the naturally supernatural life: doing the works of the kingdom of God and the contemplative life go hand-in-hand. Power and intimacy work together. I used to think they were polar opposites: contemplative Christians hid away and prayed all day while the activists were busy out in the streets doing the stuff. But I was wrong. It's not either-or, it's both-and. Jesus balanced both, producing the perfect naturally supernatural life. His life was the perfect combination of solitude and prayer and actively serving the needs of others in the power of the Holy Spirit.

I've found that in order to *"do what the Father is doing"* or, as Paul put it, *"keep in step with the Spirit,"* we must cultivate healthy souls which includes unhurrying ourselves so we can become alert to what God is doing in the hidden, small, ordinary, overlooked and unexpected. If we do so, we can learn to hear God's thoughts, speak God's words, and do God's works the way Jesus did. I'll have more to say about this in later chapters.

Where to start?

Christian philosopher and author Dallas Willard urges that we ruthlessly *unhurry* our lives. Stop living like Martha and become more like Mary! How? By harnessing your busyness and creating a *God-first schedule*. By slowing down and quieting your inner noise through the practice of spiritual exercises like solitude, silence and listening prayer. By *uncluttering your soul* --putting the things that are overwhelming, over-extending and exhausting you under Jesus' management. Start with those things that drain you of life rather than give you life. Even tiring work can be energizing and satisfying if its Spirit-initiated and driven.

Begin looking for God working in your everyday routines. You'll be surprised how much you miss out on because you don't pay attention or expect God's kingdom to be present in the ordinary and unspectacular. Finally, you might consider getting a spiritual director to help you get in touch with what God is doing in and around you. Unhurrying yourself and learning to pay attention won't be easy. It will take some time, intentionality, rearranging and getting used to, but it's well worth the effort.

God is everywhere at work, advancing his kingdom all around us, and he's inviting ordinary whosoever's that are willing to accept his invitation and arrange their lives to embrace Spirit-empowered and directed living. There aren't any prerequisites for saying yes to the invitation. The only question, it seems, is 'how bad do you want it'?

2 GETTING ALONG WITH A GHOST

How do we relate to a ghost? I've found it much trickier than connecting with the Father and Son because I was left largely to my imagination. How can we interact with the Holy Spirit and experience him in a healthy way? Many Christians find him more a source of controversy than a comfort, which causes some to be skittish and jittery around him. Although such persons don't deny the Spirit, the weirdness and excess associated with some extreme varieties of charismatic-type ministry cause them to become gun-shy and keep the Spirit him at arm's length. Still others have been burned – manipulated into trying to speak in tongues or told they weren't healed because they didn't have enough faith – and have grown cynical and disillusioned throwing the baby out with the bathwater. These people not only steer clear of Holy Spirit ministry such as healing and the prophetic but are often resistant to even the slightest hint of the Spirit's involvement.

The main ingredient

This is no small matter because, as it turns out, there is no Christian life without the Holy Spirit. Jesus made it clear that when he was gone the Spirit would be the "main ingredient" in the lives of his followers. The Spirit's not optional; he's indispensable. The Holy Spirit makes the gospel livable. He animates the Christian life.

Jesus was powerfully indwelt by the Spirit of God. Everything he did -- his birth (Luke 1:35), teaching (Luke 4:18), miracles (Acts 10:38), death (Hebrews 9:14) , resurrection (Romans 8:11) and ascension (Ephesians 1:19) -- was by the Holy Spirit. Now if Jesus himself relied completely on the Holy Spirit during his earthly life how much more must we?

But as Jesus told the Jewish leader Nicodemus, the Spirit is also mysterious-- unpredictable and sovereign like the wind (John 3:8). This makes living a life led by the Holy Ghost both essential and tricky. It takes a lot of getting used to—and a lot of practice.

Is there a way of getting past the theatrics, ignorance and fear that some have encountered in "charismatic" ministry to experience and embrace a life with the Spirit that's healthy and helpful-- a way to interact with the Spirit that's safe, sane and constructive rather than the source of uneasiness, bewilderment or mockery.? There is, and it's called being naturally supernatural.

Naturally supernatural
I first became a Christian in a Pentecostal chapel service. It was loud, lively, and very expressive. It sort of felt like getting pumped up in the locker room before the big game! Coming from a quiet Roman Catholic background, I found this Pentecostal style pretty weird. Particularly strange was the way they prayed. Folks shouted, waved their hands, and jumped around! I was told this was what it looked like when the Spirit showed up and did his thing.

At first, this rowdiness didn't matter to me. I was desperate for whatever contact with the Spirit I could get, and if it meant getting a little weird, so be it. And you know what? God did meet me and began changing my life. But I soon grew uncomfortable with what seemed to be showy, strange, and, at times, manipulative behavior. I loved Jesus and the people in the church, but I didn't like the package. It wasn't me. Eventually, I grew wary of it all and became one of those Christians that avoided the Spirit and anything that might smack of weirdness – like prophesying, praying for the sick or casting out demons – as much as possible. I would soon realize that while I may have been more comfortable, I had also lost something important…

When I ran into John Wimber, I saw something different. John wasn't interested in wowing the crowd. There was no hype, weirdness or manipulation. When he ministered, he was relaxed, comfortable, real. I was impressed with how he remained "normal" even while worshiping and praying. John called it being "naturally supernatural."

John was the same person during ministry time that he was during dinnertime! I learned that I didn't have to put on some spiritual persona, change the tone of my voice when I prayed, or get dramatic or frenzied in order for the Spirit to move. The most significant and liberating discovery was that I could just be myself, and God would still show up! Boy, did that take the pressure off! I could respond to the promptings of the Spirit in my own, authentic way. That was huge for me. My response to this freedom: *I can do that! I want to do that!* I was off and running "doing the stuff" of the kingdom, and I haven't stopped since…

Being *naturally supernatural* is a big deal to me. It's made it possible for me to relate to the Holy Spirit in a personal, healthy, constructive way and to be able to partner with him outside the church where people expect Christians to be turn-offs.

Opening up new possibilities

Being naturally supernatural has wide implications. It means everyone gets to play. You can be uniquely yourself, and God can still use you. You can act normal, and God will still show up. It relieves the pressure to perform.

It opens up ministry opportunities out in the marketplace of life, not just inside the church. Unchurched folk don't feel threatened or put-off by the Spirit because there's no weirdness, hype or manipulation. Receptivity to the gospel (and those who share it) increases dramatically. People outside the church are pleasantly surprised when they meet someone that breaks that negative stereotype of the strange, uptight, legalistic, overly critical and judgmental or just plain weird Christian. Being *naturally supernatural* opens all sorts of possibilities for sharing God's love when unnecessary weirdness is set aside and paves the way for people to actually experience God's loving and healing presence in a way that feels neither threatening nor embarrassing.

In our secular world, where often a person's only reference for the supernatural is found in Hollywood fantasy and reality TV weirdness, the comfort of God's Spirit discovered in *naturally supernatural* encounters is for many the start of a faith journey of their own.

Being naturally supernatural allows us to be wonderfully subversive the way Jesus was. When you're able to be natural and comfortable to be around, people let down their guard and open up to you, to God, and to new possibilities for their lives. It allows us to partner with God and be useful to the kingdom in all the places "religious" people are mostly useless - out in the marketplace of life.

Being naturally supernatural opens a way for us to have a positive, life-giving impact among our non-religious relatives, friends, and neighbors, in our

7

workplaces, schools, and the places we gather to relax and have fun... When we conduct ourselves in naturally supernatural ways, good things seem to happen. Those around us experience the presence and power of God right where they are in non-threatening ways that leave them with a good taste in their mouths-- and wanting more. What's more, we get to impact the most unlikely people – folks that are presently uninterested in Christianity. And when we live our lives as *cooperative friends of Jesus, creatively doing good for the sake of others by the power of the Holy Spirit*, that brings *us* joy in any number of new, refreshing and exciting ways.

It's a lifestyle

Jesus was the prototypical, naturally supernatural human. He brought the kingdom of God up-close-and-personal to ordinary, everyday folk simply by being approachable and involved in the affairs of their normal, everyday lives.

So what does a naturally supernatural lifestyle look like? When most people think of being used by God, they think of something demanding and difficult, something otherworldly and strange-- way out of their league and comfort zone. But that's not it at all. Actually, it looks like YOU when you're at your best-- relaxed, not self-conscious, being yourself, loving God, and spontaneously and creatively keeping in step with what the Spirit is doing-- being the fully empowered human being God created you to be.

Being naturally supernatural is about being alert to God's Spirit showing up in the midst of your daily routines and using you to help those around you. For my wife and me, being naturally supernatural has been mostly wrapped in the unspectacular and ordinary. It's meant simply being good neighbors. That's led to being invited into people's lives, which has often opened a natural, relaxed way of sharing our faith stories with them and opened their eyes and hearts to a God who is present and has power to be a difference-maker in their lives.

Over the years, being naturally supernatural has led to many of our neighbors becoming comfortable talking about God and even asking for prayer. A number have found faith in Jesus. You might say that the most powerful naturally supernatural thing we've done is offer friendship, hospitality, and prayer to our neighbors.

This makes perfect sense because the Holy Spirit is friendly! If you want to have a naturally supernatural impact on people, be friendly. It opens all kinds of doors for ministry.

That's the way it worked with our next-door neighbors, Terry and John (not their real names). We became good friends, often hanging out together on our back porch on warm evenings talking about life in general and our shared love of the Yankees. We got to know each other pretty well. Terry and John knew that Char and I were followers of Jesus. And we knew that they were Catholics, but our conversations about faith never went very far. Still, we could tell that they respected our beliefs very much.

One afternoon I was doing yard work when out of the corner of my eye I caught a glimpse of Terry sitting on the back stairs of her house. Her head was down and, upon a closer look, I realized she was crying. Now, I'm not one to poke my nose into other people's business, but we were friends. We had a level of trust where I felt I could infringe on what seemed like a very private moment.

"Terry, is everything okay?" She looked up and, wiping tears from her eyes, said, "Not really. I just got some bad news…"

Terry shared that she had just received the heartbreaking news from her doctor that she would not be able to have children of her own because of a physical condition that she had.

Now, if we were strangers or if she thought Char and I were weird, odd-ball Christians, what happened next would have probably never occurred. But because we were comfortable with each other, I was able to pop the question. "You know Char and I follow Jesus and believe that he can heal you. Would you let us pray for you right now?"

I don't know if she believed that Jesus could heal her or not, but because she trusted us she allowed us to pray for her right there in the backyard. We didn't make a big deal out of it, but we followed the Vineyard prayer model (see chapter eleven) and gave it our best shot. When we were through Terry thanked us and said she felt "comforted." I thought to myself, "Well, I'll settle for that."

To make a long story short-- almost twenty years later, John and Terry have three biological children!

And as a result of Terry's healing, their faith was renewed, and they've become sincere practicing Catholics.

And it all came about because we were friendly and easy to be around—and took the risk of sharing the good things we knew of Jesus with our friends.

So how do you become naturally supernatural? It's all about being open, alert, and available to the Holy Spirit. It's a matter of responding obediently to his ofttimes unexpected, even inconvenient whispers, nudges, and promptings. It's letting him custom-fit you with an *incarnational lifestyle* that looks like Jesus if he were you--a lifestyle that shows others around you what God is like by living like Jesus and doing the things he did. It's being a good neighbor the way Jesus would be a neighbor if he were you. Being a nurturing and encouraging grandparent the way Jesus would be a grandparent.

Being an excellent teacher the way Jesus would be a teacher if he taught your students. Being a competent and responsible custodian the way Jesus would be a custodian if he did your job. It can't be done in isolation. It's about living connected to Jesus while connecting with your neighbors, co-workers, and classmates--which means you'll have to get out of your cocoon and socialize and make friends. It also means living with a *purpose* – with an awareness that, as a follower of Jesus, you've been invited to participate in his mission of loving people and making the world around you a better place.

One last thing: to keep your naturally supernatural lifestyle fresh and ongoing, you'll have to keep giving away what God has freely given to you-- *his love!* Being naturally supernatural isn't a self-improvement program or a path to enjoying private spiritual experiences. It's about doing good for the sake of others by the power of the Holy Spirit, a lifestyle of Spirit-empowered friendship and service.

The Humanizer
But being naturally supernatural is more than just a relaxed, no-hype style of doing ministry. It's a way of regaining something lost, something Jesus modeled by the power of the Spirit and wants to impart to us – our full humanity. Being *naturally* supernatural means that I don't stop being human when I engage with the (supernatural) Holy Spirit. On the contrary, I become more completely human-- the way Jesus was human.

There's a story about Dallas Willard being asked what one word best described Jesus. You might expect him to answer with a word like holy, loving, or powerful. But the word he gave was "*relaxed*"! When I heard that, it made me think of John's idea of being naturally supernatural – a way of being in the world that is calm, comfortable, at ease, and unpretentious as well as anointed and powerful.

You see, the Holy Spirit is, in the words of the fourth century theologian, Athanasias, the *"rehumanizing Spirit."* His job is not to make us more religious, but to make us more human the way God intended us to be human. His work is to re-create and complete our humanity, remaking us in the image of Christ, the perfect naturally supernatural person, so we can enjoy living and co-laboring with God in his world.

This was God's intention from the beginning when he breathed his Spirit into the first human being (Gen 2:7). I don't believe we were ever meant to be religious weirdos. We were created to live fully human, naturally supernatural lives, in partnership with him.

Being naturally supernatural has become a core value of mine. This down-to-earth, honest, everyday and yet miraculous spirituality has enabled me to break the negative stereotype of weird, off-putting Christianity and practice a relaxed, natural way of exercising spiritual gifts and praying for people. And it's helped me become a more fully God-honoring, Spirit-controlled, honest-to-goodness human being, doing my best to live life like Jesus lived, doing the stuff he did. I can be myself, warts and all, and still enjoy the exhilarating and rewarding experience of God's power working in and through my life for the sake of Christ and others, making the world around me a little bit better place to live.

Reflection and Action

1. How would you describe your view of the Holy Spirit? (Scared, anxious, curious, resistant, open, etc.)

2. Mike mentions ways of doing ministry(?) that turn people off. What would do that to you and how do you think Christians can better be "naturally supernatural"?

3. Think of and share a story where you were ineffective at doing kingdom work, a failure, and a story where you did it right. What was different between the two?

4. To maintain a "naturally supernatural" lifestyle, Mike says we have to keep giving away God's love. As you pray and ask God to speak to you, does anyone come to mind that you can do this for? What do you think you can do for them to share God's love with them in a "naturally supernatural" way?

5. What will it take for you to partner with the Spirit and do the stuff Jesus did and still be yourself?

3 THE BIG HUG

Some Christians treat the Holy Spirit like their personal tour guide to exotic spiritual experiences. He's not. He's the gift of Jesus' inner life that leads us into a life far better than we could ever imagine.

Spirit-filled living is without a doubt life-giving and satisfying-- at times exhilarating-- but it's a real life with ups and downs, ebbs and flows. It's not some spiritual drug we use to break up the boredom of ordinary, unspectacular, everyday life or to make us feel good about ourselves.

When we cooperate with the Holy Spirit, he produces the fruit of Jesus' life in us--a life anchored in the love of his Heavenly Father which formed the most fully human and fruitful being to have ever lived. A life "full of grace and truth" (John 1:14).

I happen to think that receiving this love is the essential charismatic experience. I call it the "Big Hug." Yet sadly it's missing from many believers' lives leaving them insecure and incomplete.

The touch of love
I imagine all the disciples' fears kicked in when Jesus broke the news that he was leaving them. Uncertainty and danger filled the air, Put yourself in their shoes. Just imagine the confusion and anxiety that must have produced in them.

Jesus assured them that they were not being abandoned (John 14:18): they'd get plenty of assistance from another Helper (14:26) who would be just like him. Things would continue much as they were, even better (16:7). They'd know just what to do and how to do it because this Helper would give them direct access to the Father, just like Jesus had. He then added this encouragement:

In that day you will ask in my name. I'm not saying that I will ask the Father on your behalf. No, the Father himself loves you dearly because you have loved me and believed that I came from God. (John 16:26-27)

Even more amazing than having this direct access to the Father is the revelation that when we love Jesus *we* receive the love of his Father! Jesus uses the same word for love here that he used to describe the Father's love for him – *phileo* (5:20). He was promising that the same demonstrated affection that he constantly received from his Father would now be available to them as well.

Jesus' baptism (Mark 1:9-11) gives a clear picture of what the experience of receiving this love was like for him. Jesus was no superman. It's easy to think that, but the incarnational reality was that, as the Son of God come in the flesh, Jesus enjoyed no advantages over other humans. He experienced life like the rest of us. He felt human emotions like sorrow, grief and joy. He got upset at times. He tired, became hungry, and needed rest like all of us. So, when Jesus comes to the Jordan in Mark 1, he comes in human weakness and humility, likely with a sense of the difficult road ahead of him. This will be no cakewalk; he'll endure unspeakable suffering. Jesus will be asked to take on the weight of human sin in a face-off against the powers of evil on the cross. It's not a stretch to suppose that he's a bit anxious. I don't think it's too far-fetched to imagine, then, that he might be in need of some encouragement and support from his Father – a big hug.

And what happens? Jesus gets exactly what his heart requires! The Father gives him the comfort and assurance he needs. He experiences the powerful felt-presence of the Father's affection for his Son. He hears the powerful words every human needs to hear: "I love you". He receives the touch we all crave - the warm, tender touch of his Father's love as the Holy Spirit descends upon him. His heart is secured, and if there was any trace of apprehension, it melts away.

This was Jesus' *Abba experience*, what some call the central event of Jesus' earthly life, and it proved to be of critical importance. As far as we know, from this moment on, Jesus never felt that he was even an arm's length away from his Father who loved him.

By the way, I don't think Jesus' experience of the Father's love at his baptism was an isolated incident in Jesus' life. It apparently happens again and again. Take for instance, his transfiguration (Matthew 17:1-8): Jesus comes in weakness, humbly submits himself to his Father's will, and gets the Big Hug. His Father pours out his empowered affection by the Spirit, which moves Jesus forward into the next step of his mission secure and confident.

"The one who sent me is with me; he has not left me alone, for I always do what pleases him..." (John 8:29 MSG)

Jesus faced every challenge, every crisis, by walking humbly in dependence on the power of his Father's love made present by the Holy Spirit.

This was the help that Jesus was promising his disciples in the Upper Room. The Father would pour the same life-securing love into their hearts that Jesus had received at his baptism by the Spirit and enable them to continue the work his Son had begun.

This promise wasn't just for the Twelve. It extends to you and me. That same night Jesus prayed that every person who comes to love and trust him would experience the empowering love of his Father:

[20] "I am praying not only for these disciples but also for all who will ever believe in me through their message. [21] I pray that they will all be one, just as you and I are one—as you are in me, Father, and I am in you. And may they be in us so that the world will believe you sent me... O righteous Father, the world doesn't know you, but I do; and these disciples know you sent me. I have revealed you to them, and I will continue to do so. Then your love for me will be in them, and I will be in them." (John 17:20-21; 25-26)

This is great news! Jesus' ongoing ministry to us is to reveal the Father in the same way he knew the Father – as "Abba" - through the power of the Holy Spirit. That same Spirit, which communicates the Father's love, moves us beyond ourselves into (Jesus') mission!

My story...

Even though I had been following Jesus for quite some time and pastoring my second church, I had not come to know my loving Father in heaven. The tender affection of a father's love was missing in my life, which left me an insecure, angry, and defensive leader with a church on the verge of mutiny because I had offended so many of them.

I was on a retreat with several other pastors that I trusted and with whom I was very close. I confessed the mess I was in and how angry, afraid and ashamed of myself I was.

One of the pastors looked straight at me and said, "Mike, you need the blessing of your heavenly Father," and began praying that I'd receive *the spirit of adoption*. As he prayed, I began experiencing something powerful yet intimate. It was like God was breathing into me, invading a part of me that had never been touched before! A warm presence began flooding me. I was being held by a love that my earthly father could never give me. In that moment I felt like a son, not just a servant. As this was happening, my pastor friend spoke words of the Father's blessing and affirmation over me-- words that I had always longed to hear: "Mike, you're God's son. He loves you. He's proud to be your Father..." It was overwhelming. It was wonderful. I was receiving the Big Hug I had always longed for-- the warmth of the Father's *phileo* love. My heart was finally at rest. I felt safe and secure.

Looking back, I can point to that experience as the beginning of a process of gradually moving from being an insecure, impulsive, and angry servant to becoming a son and, eventually, a spiritual father to my church.

Subsequent Abba experiences have been less dramatic but have usually followed the same pattern: I am in need. The Holy Spirit comes, and I feel the warmth of the Father's loving presence and hear him speak reassuring things to me. I'm usually emotionally moved as my guilt or anxiety is dealt with. My heart is secured, enabling me to continue to move forward in life and ministry.

The Abba experience in Paul's epistles
Paul writes about this experience in Romans 5:

And hope does not put us to shame, because God's love has been poured out into our hearts through the Holy Spirit, who has been given to us. (Romans 5:5)

He's uses the term "poured out", commonly used in Pentecostal circles to describe the ultimate charismatic experience! In Romans 8 Paul again describes experiencing the Father's love though the work of the Holy Spirit. There he gives us a picture of how the Spirit convinces us that our Father in heaven actually loves us as true sons and daughters, making our *adoption* a reality that we can experience.

For those who are led by the Spirit of God are the children of God. The Spirit you received does not make you slaves, so that you live in fear again; rather, the Spirit you received brought about your adoption to sonship. And by him we cry, "Abba, Father." The Spirit himself testifies with our spirit that we are God's children. Now if we are children, then we are heirs—heirs of God and co-heirs with Christ, if indeed we share in his sufferings in order that we may also share in his glory. (Romans 8:14-17)

The Greek word Paul uses for adoption literally means "placing as a son" which captures something of the experience of the Spirit's work in bringing us into the presence of our heavenly Father. This is more than a theological concept. Paul's language is vivid and experiential: we cry, "Abba, Father," a cry that is intimate and intense.

The Holy Spirit touches us in such a way that we're made aware that we belong and are accepted; we actually feel the Big Hug. This is a powerful spiritual experience beyond our minds that can be emotional and physical as well. I believe this is what Jesus felt at his baptism.

In other words, what happened to Jesus happens to us. The Holy Spirit comes upon us and places us in the presence of our heavenly Father where we can feel his loving touch and hear his voice of love. The experience secures our hearts so we can join him in the family business of advancing the kingdom of God on earth as it is in heaven.

This is going to raise some eyebrows, but try this on for size: Could Pentecost have been a ten-megaton Big Hug (Acts 2:1-13)? So big that it exploded the Church into existence? Could the wind, tongues of fire, and "drunkenness" have been a huge dose of God's love being poured out by the Spirit-- like an exuberant father playfully roughhousing with his children? Well, maybe that's a stretch, but here we have the disciples apparently experiencing the same felt presence and power of God that Jesus experienced at his baptism, their being called and empowered to share in the same relationship Jesus enjoyed with his Father and with the same result – the community of the Spirit is launched into mission to the world (see Acts 1:8).

You and I

In the course of our journeys with God, we will have many varied spiritual experiences-- some subtle, some dramatic. The Abba experience is ongoing; it's part of a process.

The Father by his Spirit will continue to give us the Big Hug, pouring out his love, again and again, over and over, touching us with the warmth of his tender affection, speaking words of support and encouragement to our hearts, crowding out our unbelief and mistrust, healing our heart-wounds and insecurities, until our identity is based on the truth that we are unconditionally loved by our heavenly Father, no strings attached, rather than on the devil's lies and past hurts-- until it's a settled fact in our hearts that we are beloved children of our heavenly Father.

Wherever you are in your experience of the Father's love, you can always ask for more. The Spirit will descend on you to do the work he always does-- bring you into the presence of your heavenly Father, bear witness to, convince and assure you of his love for you.

This reminds me of Paul's prayer for the Ephesians:

When I think of all this, I fall to my knees and pray to the Father,[a] the Creator of everything in heaven and on earth. I pray that from his glorious, unlimited resources he will empower you with inner strength through his Spirit. Then Christ will make his home in your hearts as you trust in him. Your roots will grow down into God's love and keep you strong. And may you have the power to understand, as all God's people should, how wide, how long, how high, and how deep his love is. May you experience the love of Christ, though it is too great to understand fully. Then you will be made complete with all the fullness of life and power that comes from God. (Ephesians 3:14-19)

Reflection and Action

1. Receiving the "big hug," or experiencing the Father's love, is a profound experience that is different for many people. Have you encountered God in this way? If so, describe that experience. If not, explain your feelings on the idea.

2. How would explain the relationship between love, grace, and truth? Why is there often tension between these three?

3. What keeps people from receiving God's love? Have you ever resisted his love and if so, why?

4. The Apostle Paul wrote that the Holy Spirit pours out God's love into our hearts (ROM. 5:5) and that our love for others comes from the Spirit as well (Col. 1:8). How do you define love and what are a few of the most loving acts you have personally witnessed?

5. What would experiment more of God's love look like for you? How can Jesus meet your immediate and long-term needs?

6. "Doing" love can be risky. How have you seen love and faith work together in your life? How might this activate more if the Spirit's work in and through your life?

4 MAKING SENSE OF THE BAPTISM

Several years ago, we took a friend to her first ever baseball game. The Yankees were rallying so the opposing manager went to the mound and removed the starting pitcher to bring in a reliever. Yankee fans were cheering wildly. As the pitcher walked slowly back to the dugout with his head down, our friend asked, "Did we just vote him out of the game?" I laughed and explained to her that there was no voting in baseball. She was witnessing baseball live and firsthand, but her lack of understanding of the game caused her to misread what was going on. Her experience was real, but her conclusion was wrong.

I'm afraid that something similar is the case when it comes to describing the baptism of the Holy Spirit. The experience is real, but our understanding and explanation leave much to be desired and, in some cases, are simply wrong. As John Wimber, the founder of the Vineyard movement, once said, "From time to time we will have a valid experience with an invalid label... my perception is that that is what has occurred with the issue of the baptism of the Holy Spirit..."

My basement baptism

I became a follower of Jesus while a resident of Teen Challenge in Brooklyn, a Christian a drug program. The people that ran it were Pentecostals. When I gave my life to Christ and was baptized in water, I thought I was good to go. "Not so fast" they told me. There was something more I needed, called *the baptism of the Holy Spirit*. This "extra" experience supposedly made certain spiritual benefits available to me-- things like holiness, boldness, and power to witness and even perform signs and wonders. The necessary initial sign of this experience, according to them, was speaking in a weird language they called "tongues."

As I understood it, these extra benefits could only occur after I had spoken in tongues. Tongues to them was a big deal. They made it sound like tongue-talkers had something more real and alive than those that didn't and pointed to the "deadness" of non-tongues-talking churches as proof.

Now, I wasn't sure about this tongues business, but I figured I could use all the extra help I could get, so I went for it...

Legit or con job?

One evening not long after I heard about the "baptism of the Holy Spirit," a guest minister came to speak at our chapel service whose specialty was helping people receive this Holy Spirit baptism. During the service the invitation was given to come forward and receive prayer. I decided to give it a shot. No sooner did I get to the altar than I found myself surrounded by people shouting loudly into my ear in tongues. I was annoyed and very uncomfortable. Then the guest minister began prompting me to repeat some gibberish over and over after her, which made me even more uncomfortable. I was freaked out! I went on red alert. And then I felt like a fool! How could this be God? I went back to my room, disillusioned and angry!

That night I couldn't sleep. Was this "baptism of the Holy Spirit" business just a sham? I had to find out. So after everyone was asleep, I went down to the basement. I paced around the room in a circle, praying out loud, "Jesus, if the Holy Spirit baptism is real, prove it to me." I continued circling and praying for a little while. But then I began hearing that same strange babble inside my head that I had heard in the service earlier that evening. At first, I thought it was my imagination or maybe just my recollection of what I'd heard just a few hours ago. I tried to ignore it, but it persisted. Then I surprised myself: I took a risk and decided to speak out what I was hearing in my head. I figured, what the heck? I was alone. Who would know?

At first what came out of my mouth was just babble. But as I kept it up, it started to form into what sounded like a crude language. Although it was Greek to me, I sensed it was from God. So there I was, walking in circles and speaking in tongues, and the more I did it, the stronger I sensed God's presence. Despite the strangeness of it all, I knew I was on the right track, so I kept it up.

Contrary to what I had thought it would be like, I discovered that speaking in tongues wasn't like being taken over by some alien force.

I could control it. I could start and stop any time I wanted. I could be as loud or quiet as I wanted. Over the next few days and weeks, the more I prayed in this strange language, the more developed and polished it became. I had my own personal prayer language at my disposal whenever I felt the need to use it. When I say, "personal prayer language," I'm referring to my private use of tongues when I pray. There are times when I pray I'm overwhelmed and at a loss for words to express myself. My use of the English language is not enough. This is where the personal gift of tongues comes in handy.

The evidence
It wasn't just the tongues. There were other indications that something real and helpful had happened that night in the basement. I didn't suddenly become a spiritual giant. I still had my same basic struggles with temptation and sin as before. I still needed rely on God's grace and forgiveness each day to carry on. But what it did do was turn me into a more confident and able servant! I had received power for service.

I also had a greater sense of God's presence and power in my life. I was more aware of him at work in and around me. I began sharing my story with others more confidently and convincingly. But what was most apparent to me was that a strong sense of mission took hold of my life. It was no longer enough for me to merely go to church, stay out of trouble, and get to heaven. I suddenly had an intense desire to serve Christ and his cause. I was convinced I had been saved to serve. Service became life-giving, joyful, and, most importantly, fruitful.

Questioning the baptism
Despite experiencing baptism in the Holy Spirit in what was essentially the Pentecostal way, I was still puzzled. The more familiar I became with Jesus, the Bible, and Christian living, the more convinced I became that my Pentecostal brothers and sisters had gotten the Spirit baptism experience wrong. I began questioning their explanation and expectations.

For instance, I kept running into faithful, saintly, powerfully anointed and gifted believers that hadn't had this second baptism experience the way Pentecostals did: they had never spoken in tongues. Yet they claimed to be Spirit-filled and empowered. And how could I doubt it?

They prayed effectively for the sick, prophesied, received dreams and visions, the same as Pentecostals did. I was confused. Why did Pentecostals insist that these other benefits and kinds of empowerment could only occur after a person had spoken in tongues? I couldn't deny the evidence to the contrary. Could it be that Pentecostals were overstating the importance of the experience of speaking in tongues? I suspected this was the case. The experience was real, but our doctrine and teaching were faulty.

So how do I explain that I spoke in tongues when I prayed for the baptism in that basement? It remains a puzzle. I'm not sure . I find Acts not entirely clear on the relationship between believing in Jesus, the baptism of the Spirit, and speaking in tongues. I don't see a precise pattern. In Acts 2, the hundred and twenty (Acts 1:15) receive the Holy Spirit with the "initial evidence" of tongues (2:4). In the case of the Samaritans in Acts 8, they believe first in Jesus but receive the empowering Spirit subsequently (8:16). When the apostles pray, something definitely happens, Simon the sorcerer witnessed something (8:18), but we're left to our imaginations as to what it was. At Cornelius's house in Acts 10, the group gathered receives the gospel and the baptism of the Spirit with tongues while Peter is talking-- as one experience! In Acts 19, the Ephesians receive the full message of Christ and the empowering of the Spirit with the evidence of both tongues and prophecy. In the end, we're not given a clear pattern in Acts for the timing and "evidence" of the baptism of the Spirit: it occurs concurrently with salvation, subsequently, after salvation, with the evidence of tongues, with unspecified evidence, with the evidence of tongues and prophecy. So personally I play it loose.

The way I see it, the Holy Spirit cannot be boxed up. He likes to color outside the lines. Jesus said he's a "free spirit," like the wind (John 3). His ways cannot be reduced to a set of principles, steps, or methods-- or even doctrines.

Because of this, I don't hold on to my explanations of spiritual experiences or phenomena too tightly. There's a great deal of mystery that goes along with all of this, so I don't let these explanations form my theology or doctrine. As best as I can, I base them on Scripture and try to avoid being dogmatic.

Dip and dye

The word "baptism" comes from the ancient textile trade and was used to describe the process of dying cloth. The cloth was "baptized" in a vat of dye, and this dipping, immersing, or soaking changed its color.

Baptism describes a process where an agent, such as dye, has the power to change an object through its being soaked (baptized).

This is a helpful picture of the work of the Holy Spirit in immersing a believing individual in a whole new reality as a result of Christ's death and resurrection. When I made the decision to follow Christ, the Bible says things changed: I was brought out of darkness and into his light (1Peter 2:9) ... transferred from death to life (Romans 6:4)... rescued out from under the control of sin and death and brought into the sphere of the Spirit's control... incorporated into the spiritual community called the Body of Christ, the Church (1 Corinthians 12:13).

My immersion in the realm or control of the Spirit changed my state of being and gave me a new status. I was now a new creation (2 Cor. 5:17), no longer alienated (Col. 1:21-23), no longer dead in my sin (Eph 2:4-5), tasting the life of the age to come (Heb 6:5), alive to God (Rom 6:11), a citizen of his kingdom (Phil 3:20), an adopted and beloved member of my heavenly Father's family (Eph 1:5), co-heir with Christ (Rom 8:16—17), part of a royal priesthood (1 Pet 2:5), anointed with his Spirit (1 John 2:20). That's some life-changing soaking!

This initial baptism in the Spirit occurs right at the start, at salvation. But all its benefits may not be immediate. The same is true of marriage: its full benefits are not immediately realized at the altar the moment the bride and groom exchange vows and say, "I do." They come through a relational process that takes place over time. Some of the benefits of salvation are immediate-- like forgiveness, adoption, and incorporation into the Body of Christ. Others are activated and actualized over time-- like the fruit of the Spirit and exercise of spiritual gifts.

Fillings
I've continued to have experiences with the Spirit since that episode in the basement. Some have been rather dramatic, but most have been of the more unspectacular variety, real and helpful nonetheless.

These experiences – whether we call them "baptisms" or "fillings" isn't important – have helped me activate or gain greater access to a Spirit-empowered life. In Ephesians, Paul emphasizes a state of living under the control of the Holy Spirit rather than having occasional experiences (5:18).. The word Paul uses in this verse, translated "be filled", carries the idea of living under the constant influence of another. In other words, Paul is saying, *"Live constantly under the influence and direction of the Spirit."* This condition of being "filled" isn't a matter of me getting more of the Spirit. He gets more of me--more access to my life, more of my cooperation.

I submit, yield, relinquish control, and trust him so I can continue to stay in step with him (Galatians 5:25).

So, while there is an initial baptism into Christ at salvation, there can be many fillings or experiences that make more room in our lives for the Spirit to exercise control over us, and none of them have to be accompanied by any other specific manifestation. They may have these features, or they may not. What's important is the fruit of empowered, Christ-like living and service.

I'm going to go out on a limb here: do you suppose Jesus' baptism and transfiguration may have been two of the more spectacular examples of fillings he experienced during his time on earth? I think so. They both came at critical junctures in his ministry where he was facing enormous pressure and was perhaps in need of the encouragement and empowering of the Spirit. These could have been moments when he accessed more of the benefits of being the Beloved of the Father. To my mind, this isn't such a stretch since Jesus was also a prototype of a new kind of Spirit-controlled human being, leading the way for you and me.

Reflection and Action

1. Have you heard the phrase "baptism of the Spirit"? What does the phrase bring to mind? If you have had a similar experience, how would you describe it in your own words?

2. Read Acts 2 and 1 Corinthians 12-14. How would you describe the gift of tongues? In light of the Apostle Paul's teaching in 1 Corinthians 14:1, how would you describe your desire for spiritual gifts in general and the gift of tongues specifically?

3. William Seymour, an African American preacher and early Pentecostal leader, said that love is the primary sign of Spirit baptism. What other evidences do you believe would demonstrate one has been "baptized" or "filled" by the Holy Spirit?

4. Ephesians 5:18 teaches us to be "filled with the Spirit," an ongoing experience, not a one-time event. Mike describes this experience as being less about receiving "more of the Spirit" and more about the Spirit having more "access" to our lives, more of our cooperation. What would this look like in your own life?

5 HANDLING SPIRITUAL GIFTS WITH CARE

The Greatest American Hero

Back in the eighties there was a TV series called, "The Greatest American Hero." It followed the adventures of Ralph Hinkley, a schoolteacher who is given a suit by aliens which endows him with super powers in order to battle injustice and crime. Unfortunately, Ralph loses the instruction manual that came with the suit and has to figure out how to use its powers by trial and error as he goes along. Without the instructions, he never really gets the hang of using his powers and makes a mess of things week after week. Ralph's experiences in flying yield particularly comical results as he tries to control the suit, screaming like a banshee in mid-air and suffering regular embarrassing crash landings.

The Greatest American Hero comes to mind when I think of how the Holy Spirit imparts spiritual power and abilities to mere mortals who are saved by grace. Though they're given to us with no strings attached, we can't possibly expect good results if we fail to follow the directions. Divine power comes with instructions, and they must be obeyed. If we fail to follow them and fly by the seat of our pants instead, we, like Ralph, will suffer our share of crash landings.

The lesson of the Corinthians

Spiritual gifts should come with warning labels that state, "Spiritual gifts can be dangerous. Follow directions carefully." For reasons I'll never fully understand, God gives his children access to his power without regard to merit, accomplishments, success or maturity. Spiritual gifts are pure grace, expressions of his extravagantly generous favor (1 Pet 4:10). These gifts are not rewards for meritorious behavior or awards for special achievements. They can't be earned.

27

They can only be received. Because of this, I like to call them "grace-gifts."

Just as every follower of Christ is a recipient of grace, each and every follower of Christ is given gifts (1 Cor. 12:1,7; Eph. 4:7). Spiritual gifts are not just for superstars. They're also not given for the purpose of self-improvement. They're God's power for the rendering of humble, loving, sacrificial, Christ-like service to others. They're tools for the building up of Christ's Church and for joining him in the mission of seeing God's kingdom come on earth as it is in heaven.

Like superhero suits, spiritual gifts have power - power that, if mishandled, can make quite a mess of things and even be harmful. This is apparently what happened in the case of the Corinthians who failed to pay attention to the instruction manual for their "suits." Their misguided views of spirituality and penchant for the more miraculous gifts turned their gatherings into a free for all to see who was more spiritual than the other.

The apostle Paul was called upon to straighten things out, and he lays out the most extensive set of directions in the Bible for using spiritual gifts in a few chapters of a letter he wrote to the Corinthians (1 Corinthians 12-14). Paul starts off in chapter twelve with the concept of the church as a body and calls for unity amid the diversity of its many component parts. Although there are a variety of gifts, proper to each part of the body, they're to be exercised interdependently rather than competitively:

A spiritual gift is given to each of us as a means of helping the entire church (12:7, TLB)

This is a picture of teamwork: *Now all of you together are Christ's body, and each of you is a separate and necessary part of it. (12:27)*

There are to be no show-offs, no celebrities, no competition or jealously, no spiritual haves and have-nots, no spiritual elitism. In the Body of Christ no one member is more important than the other. Every member is Spirit-driven. Every member is Spirit-dependent. Every member is necessary. Every member makes a contribution. Every member counts.

In chapter fourteen Paul discusses the gifts of tongues and prophecy and zeroes in on the problem at hand: the issue of disorder in the Corinthian church's gatherings, which stems from their "super-spiritual" approach to the gifts.

At the end of the chapter, Paul writes,

Well, my brothers and sisters, let's summarize. When you meet together, one will sing, another will teach, another will tell some special revelation God has given, one will speak in tongues, and another will interpret what is said. But everything that is done must strengthen all of you (14:26).

Practically speaking, this means that only things which edify the whole body should be allowed in the church's gatherings, and in order to edify the church they must be intelligible to all. Private, exotic experiences in public services only benefit the individual having them. While he or she may be having a meaningful engagement with the Lord (who's to know?), those observing are left scratching their heads or, worse, turned off by the strangeness of the display. Only manifestations that are broadly understandable are of benefit and should be encouraged in the congregation. Paul also insists on a certain corporate etiquette—a politeness that's consistent with God's character to keep things orderly and sensible. If something is not intelligible or is basically disruptive to the gathering, it's to be controlled and kept from dominating the attention of the group. This framework presupposes continuing pastoral guidance in the exercise of spiritual gifts and even correction when necessary.

Sandwiched between these two sections on gifts is Paul's magnificent love chapter:

If I could speak all the languages of earth and of angels, but didn't love others, I would only be a noisy gong or a clanging cymbal. ² If I had the gift of prophecy, and if I understood all of God's secret plans and possessed all knowledge, and if I had such faith that I could move mountains, but didn't love others, I would be nothing. ³ If I gave everything I have to the poor and even sacrificed my body, I could boast about it; but if I didn't love others, I would have gained nothing. (13:1-3)

This seems like a digression, but it isn't. It's the heart of Paul's case. No matter how dazzling and impressive a spiritual gift or manifestation may be, it's worthless unless it's being used to express God's selfless love in some way. The Corinthians are to excel at building each other up with their spiritual gifts as an application of love. Spiritual power is real power, and when misused it can do harm. The only really safe way to handle spiritual gifts is under the influence of—and on the model of-- God's selfless, self-surrendering love. Only as we are clothed in Christ and his love (Romans 13:14) are we properly attired in his superhero suit and safe to use his power. We're talking about character here.

Gifting and character are not necessarily linked. They don't automatically go hand in hand. Anointing does not validate godly character. Gifts don't necessarily signal God's approval of the gifted. Just because a person is gifted doesn't mean he or she is spiritually mature or possesses an upright character. Just ask Samson and king Saul. Gifting and anointing are linked only to God's grace -- free, unconditional, unearned, undeserved grace.

We live in a celebrity culture. People are attracted to the display of power. When it comes to handling spiritual power and all the recognition --and even stardom—that it attracts, I've found that the greater the gifting or anointing, the greater the need for character to guard against all the temptation that comes along with it.

Christ-like character is essential for the heathly, long-term use of spiritual gifts. It's foundational. Character or the fruit of the Spirit is the "undergarment" that must be worn with the suit of spiritual gifting and anointing. Without it, the suit never fits or works right. We all have character flaws of various sorts. No one is perfect. But the thing that sets those who are headed for trouble apart from others is what is being done about those flaws—are they being brought to Jesus's attention so he can help remediate them? It is those who don't attend to--or even make excuses for the persistence of their character flaws that will ruin themselves and hurt others in the process. Everyone is invited--encouraged--to pursue spiritual gifts (1 Cor 14:1, 39), and everyone has flaws, but those who abide in Jesus see those cracks addressed.

How is this fruit developed? Jesus gave the following instructions. We do well to heed them:

I am the vine; you are the branches. Those that remain in me and I in them, will produce much fruit. For apart from me you can do nothing… I have loved you even as the Father has loved me. Remain in my love. When you obey me, you remain in my love, just as I obey my Father and remain in his love. (John 15:5, 9-10)

It's about abiding in Christ-- remaining in an intimate relationship of dependence on him. It's not rocket science. It's continued childlike love, trust and obedience that builds character and safeguards the exercise of spiritual gifts so they build-up and benefit the body of Christ.

Reflection and Action

1. The Bible teaches that *everyone* receives spiritual gifts from the Holy Spirit (1 Cor. 12:1,7; Eph. 4:7; 1 Pet. 4:10-11), why do you think many people feel they do *not* have spiritual gifts?

2. How would you describe the *purpose* of spiritual gifts?

3. In what ways have you seen spiritual gifts carried out in loving ways? How about unloving ways?

4. Mike says that in order to properly exercise spiritual gifts, we need to the foundational "fruit of the Spirit" (Gal. 5:22-23), which comes as we "abide in Christ." What does abiding in Christ look like in your everyday life?

6 DISCOVERING YOUR GRACE-GIFTS

God gives every member of the body of Christ at least one spiritual gift (1Cor. 12:7). Sadly, these gifts often remain unwrapped because many Christians are unaware that they're in their lives waiting to be discovered and used. How do we find out what our spiritual gifts are and begin exercising them?

A relational feature to gifts
The process of discovering spiritual gifts is more like falling in love than learning algebra. There's a relational dynamic to it. You don't have to understand love to fall in love. Similarly, you don't have to understand much of anything about the theology or mechanics of spiritual gifts in order to experience and exercise them. We become acquainted with spiritual gifts and gain facility in exercising them through personal relationship with the Giver of gifts and participation in community, the body of Christ. Spiritual gifts are "caught" through modeling and impartation at least as much as they're taught. Like love, the more I experience the gifts, the more familiar they become; and the more familiar I become with them, the more maturely I exercise them and more deeply I can enjoy the satisfaction of operating in them.

Discovering your spiritual gifts
So how do we find out what our spiritual gifts are? First off, spiritual gifts are not a private, personal experience. They're not discovered, developed or exercised in seclusion. Those all happen in community as we serve and care for one another and our neighbors. As we see from 1 Corinthians, spiritual gifts are community-building tools.

Here are four things you may want to try that I think will help you discover your spiritual gifts in community:

First, make yourself available and useful. Serve, serve, and serve some more. Spiritual gifts are tools for serving so you can expect to discover yours in the context of serving. And, as you serve, don't be afraid to experiment with gifts. Try using the ones you think you may have. Pray for the sick. Engage in acts of generosity and kindness. Care for the poor. If an experiment in using one of the gifts fails, it's not fatal. Don't be discouraged. You're just narrowing your list of possibilities.

Second, as you serve, be alert for what I call the "alive" feeling. This is the sense of exhilaration or buoyancy you get when you're exercising your spiritual gift(s). It's the feeling that 'fed' Jesus and left him so satisfied and energized after his conversation with the Samaritan woman (John 4:31-34). It never fails that I feel most complete and whole as a person when I'm operating in my gifting. I'm at my best. Exercising spiritual gifts is uplifting, satisfying, and joyful because it helps us become our true selves. We're tapping into God's image stamped within us. We're becoming more like the one who gives the best gifts of all – our Father in heaven. So, you can expect to feel energized. Pay attention to that.

My third suggestion is pretty obvious: examine and evaluate the outcomes. Spiritual gifts get results. People with the gift of healing see the sick recover quite regularly. When those with the gift of teaching unpack truth and ideas, people learn. Nonbelievers are converted when the gift of evangelism is in operation. Spiritual gifts, when first discovered, don't come full blown in a mature package; they need to be developed over time, But you can still look for some indication of positive results. If you suspect you may have a certain spiritual gift, you should be seeing clear, concrete outcomes when you attempt to practice that gift. If not, there's a good chance you don't have that gift.

Fourth, expect unsolicited confirmation from others-- and not just from your best friends. If you're truly gifted in some area of ministry, you can anticipate getting positive feedback, especially from your pastoral leaders. This is, of course, assuming you're actively participating in a local church community where you are known. If those who are most familiar with you don't recognize your gifting, there's a good chance you're not gifted in that particular area. Your community—in this as in many other things—helps you avoid the potential deception of your own subjectivity.

33

But again, don't get discouraged. Keep desiring gifts, keep serving, keep experimenting, and honestly assess the results, and you'll eventually discover and develop the gifts that God has given you.

How spiritual gifts are developed
Spiritual gifts are more caught than taught. The baptism of the Holy Spirit (Acts 1:8)-- where power for service is either imparted through the laying on of hands or released sovereignly with no human involvement-- seems to play a part in making the gifts operational in a person's life, like it did for the lives of the first deacons in the Jerusalem church and Paul in Acts (Acts 6:6; 9:17).

As I mentioned, gifts are never imparted full-blown but rather in "embryonic" form. They mature over time with nurture and use as well as a deepening of our relationship with Jesus. There's a great need for pastoral training.

I have found the "show and tell" method most useful in gift formation:
  -a gifted trainer models the gift, then explains it
  -you try it with the gifted trainer looking on and discuss it some more
  -you do it on your own
  -after some practice of your own, you train someone else

Development and growth come with practice which includes making mistakes and even failing at times. This means dumping perfectionism and the need for control. As your tolerance for discomfort, messiness, and taking risks increases, so will your childlikeness and spontaneity—and your freedom in partnering with the Spirit in the exercise of your gift.

Testing gifts
What about testing and regulating spiritual gifts? Some advocate a hands-off approach in order to avoid resisting or quenching the Spirit. I think this is a mistake. So did the Apostle Paul, as his letter to the Corinthians makes plain: "for God is not a God of disorder put of peace" (1 Cor 14:33). To insure maximum helpfulness, the exercise of spiritual gifts in local churches calls for hands-on pastoral care as well as correction when needed.

Here's four guiding questions for affirming the expression of a particular spiritual gift in the congregation's gathering I've found helpful: 1) Is this manifestation intelligible or is it confusing? 2) Is it biblical? 3) Does it have God-honoring and community-building consequences? and4) Is it loving in a Christ-resembling fashion?

The discernment and wisdom that this kind of pastoral leadership and care requires comes with prayer, a working knowledge of God's Word, and, of course, experience over time.

Wise pastoral oversight doesn't hinder the Spirit. It creates the sort of safe, healthy environment necessary for the beneficial and constructive discovery, development, and operation of spiritual gifts in a congregation.

Spiritual Experiences

Let me close with a word on how we experience spiritual gifts. The Bible isn't a textbook on spiritual experiences. It doesn't explain, analyze or dissect them for us. The writers of the Bible took the existence of God and spiritual experiences for granted. It never occurred to them that they had to. The supernatural was just part of their worldview. They didn't give much thought to how it worked, the same way most people today don't know how their cable TV works. They just accept it as a normal part of their lives. So what I'm attempting to explain about the experience and operation of spiritual gifts isn't based on extended discussions of spiritual experience found in the Bible. It's based mostly on personal experience and observation-- so take it with a grain of salt.

What's it like to be operating in a spiritual gift? Honestly, I've experienced them in lots of different of ways. There are times when teaching it's felt like, a "measure of faith" welling up inside me (Romans 12:3). I've experienced the gift of service and helps as a sense of burden. At times the gift of healing has bubbled up as a surge of power from within (Mark 5:30). The gift of word of knowledge has come as a gentle whisper or nudging in my spirit. There have been times I've experienced the discernment of spirits as an internal signal of sorts going off in my spirit that gives me insight to the source of whatever is going on (Acts 16:18). On occasion there's been no thought or feeling to it at all--just a burst of spontaneity, like automatic speech, without forethought or preparation. But it always involves an element of risk and some element of trust in, familiarity with, attentiveness to, or cooperation with the Spirit.

Mystery

The more I experience the Holy Spirit in my life, the more prominent mystery becomes. Why spiritual gifts? Why has God chosen to place his treasures in the hands of such weak and imperfect vessels as you and I? Why do they work in such puzzling ways? Why do they appear to be so unpredictable and enigmatic?

I like what Watchman Nee has to say concerning God and mystery in his book, *The Normal Christian Life*:

"There is nothing stereotyped about God's dealings with His children. Therefore, we must not by our prejudices and preconceptions make watertight compartments for the working out His Spirit, either in our own lives or in the lives of others. We must leave God free to work as He wills and to leave what evidence He pleases of the work He does."

Amen…

Reflection and Action

1. When you see the word "mystery" connected to the Holy Spirit, what comes to mind and why?

2. Looking at lists like 1 Cor. 12, Rom. 12:6-8, Eph. 4:11, and 1 Pet. 4:10-11, what are examples of spiritual gifts you have operated in? How did you "discover" these?

3. What would it look like if you made yourself more available to the Holy Spirit? Specifically speaking, how could you serve in a local church or ministry that would give you opportunities to learn about spiritual gifts?

4. Based on previous experiences you've had, what would you say you are passionate about when it comes to helping people? What makes you come alive? What spiritual gift might be attached to this passion?

5. Mike suggests that we can "grow" in our use and maturity with spiritual gifts and that they aren't immediately "imparted full blown." How does this change or challenge your assumption about spiritual gifts?

6. What are you doing to help develop and mature your spiritual gift(s)? Ask a group of people who know you what spiritual gifts *they* think you have and discuss it with them.

7 IN-THE-MOMENT MINISTRY

Remember the Jim Carrey movie *Bruce Almighty* about a down-on-his-luck TV reporter who complains to God that He's not doing his job right? Bruce gets the chance to try being God for a week and immediately begins misusing his supernatural power and making a mess of things. He's able to perform miraculous signs and wonders at a snap of his finger, but the results are disastrous. When he lassos the moon and pulls it closer to earth in order to romance his girlfriend, he causes a tsunami in Japan. He almost loses his mind when he begins to receive millions of prayers so he settles on the simple solution of saying "yes" to every request. This results in 400,000 people winning the New York lottery (a prize worth $17 each once divided) which causes a riot in the streets. At first the thought of having the sort of God-like power that Bruce gets might seem cool, but it would probably get us into all sorts of trouble, too.

There are a lot of people who think that since Jesus was God he went around performing miracles on a whim--whenever, wherever and however he wanted--more or less the way Bruce did, but without the mess. But that's not how Jesus explained it. Something else was going on-- something that opens up the possibility for ordinary folk like you and me to join him in doing some of these amazing things!

In John chapter 5, Jesus and his disciples pass by a place in Jerusalem where lots of desperate people gathered. It was a shrine of sorts where the sick and infirm crowded around a pool waiting for an angel to help one of them. As they pass through, Jesus notices one invalid in particular, whom we find out has been waiting around for quite some time.

Jesus goes over to the man and heals him with a command: "Get up!

Pick up your mat and walk."

Now it happens to be the Sabbath. By healing the man Jesus breaks a law prohibiting "work" on the Sabbath, and this gets him in trouble with the religious leaders (John 5:16).

They confront him and, in defending himself, Jesus reveals how and why he performed this miraculous work that they're all upset about:

17 In his defense Jesus said to them, "My Father is always at his work to this very day, and I too am working... Very truly I tell you, the Son can do nothing by himself; he can do only what he sees his Father doing, because whatever the Father does the Son also does. 20 For the Father loves the Son and shows him all he does. Yes, and he will show him even greater works than these, so that you will be amazed. (John 5:17-20)

There's a lot going on in this passage, but I want to focus on what Jesus explains as the key to his effective ministry because, as it turns out, it will be the key to ours as well.

Have you ever noticed how so many of Jesus' miracles appear to be unscripted and impromptu? They often seem to have occurred as he was on the way someplace or while he was in the middle of doing something else-- interruptions even, like the time a sick woman touched his cloak in a crowd (Luke 8:42-44), the time a the paralyzed man was lowered through the roof by his friends in the middle of Jesus' teaching (Luke 5:17-20), or the time that the blind man was making a scene on the side of the road to Jericho as Jesus passed by (Mark 10:46-52). In this passage where Jesus heals the lame man a the pool it seems like the same sort of thing is going on.

But as is often the case with Jesus, there's more going on here than meets the eye. What appear to be spur-of-the-moment actions are actually not. Something else is going on that catches Jesus' attention. This is an example of what I call *in-the-moment* ministry.

As his critics question Jesus, he shares his guiding principle—how he, as a human, did the miracles that he did:

"My Father is always working, and so am I." (v.17)

Despite what you might expect, Jesus didn't do his own thing.

39

He was involved in his family's business: establishing the kingdom of God *on earth as it is in heaven*. He was working along with his Father. As a human being, Jesus perfectly understood his human limitations:

"...the Son can do nothing by himself. He does only what he sees the Father doing. Whatever the Father does, the Son also does." (v. 19)

He understood that he wasn't on his own and couldn't act independently. He could only do what his Father authorized him to do by the power of the Spirit. So when Jesus sensed what his Father was up to, he simply joined in. It could have been any number of promptings-- something that caught his eye, a whisper, a nudge in his spirit, a feeling or an inner vision. Whichever way his Father got his attention, Jesus was alert, submitted and dependent enough to only do what he "saw" or sensed his Father doing. This was the key to his great authority: he and his Father always acted together. Jesus' actions had the full weight of the kingdom behind them.

Of course, it didn't hurt that Jesus was the perfectly sinless Son of God. There was no interference from sinful habits to distort his hearing like we experience. There was nothing to get in the way of Jesus' absolute trust in his Father—something we struggle with. The Holy Spirit had complete access to and control of his life. He didn't resist like we often do. The Father and Jesus were constantly in each other's presence enjoying themselves.

"For the Father loves the Son and shows him everything he is doing." (v.20)

As a result, Jesus always did what pleased the Father and only spoke out what the Father shared with him. This was the dynamic behind Jesus' miraculous works. So this healing at the pool wasn't as random as it appeared. There were lots of people hanging around that needed healing-- why this one man? Was he more deserving than the others? Couldn't Jesus have just as easily healed all the sick that were there?

In this moment, for whatever reason, the Father was busy at work in this particular man's life. And because Jesus was in tune with his Father, this particular man caught his attention. Apparently, Jesus listened to his Father's instructions and obeyed them. This released healing power in the man's life and produced the miracle.

In-the-moment ministry appears to be the usual way Jesus operated.

It was the secret of his miraculous ministry as well as the early church's (see Acts 3 for an account of Peter and John's healing of a lame man near another gate in Jerusalem), and it can be ours as well-- as Jesus' apprentices following his example.

"Just as the Father has sent me, I am sending you." (John 20:21)

As his disciples we are invited into a similar relationship of intimacy and communication with the Father by the Spirit. We are given the same tools and the same relationship as the Father's beloved children – as friends not servants – that allow us to operate in the same way as Jesus – doing what the Father is doing.

Of course, it's more of a challenge for us because we don't hear as well as Jesus, and we don't trust the Father the way Jesus did. We often miss the boat. Yet, even if imperfectly, we too, can do what the Father is doing.

If we'll begin to pay attention like Jesus did and realize that God is at work all around us and that he has invited us to take part in that work, our job becomes clear-cut: discern what God is doing and join in on the fun. It's a matter of "seeing" what God is doing in the moment and believing that he has authorized and empowered us to do it along with him. You might feel anxious and in over your head, but Jesus promised that the Spirit would be right there with us to help (Luke 12:11-12; John 14:12).

Maybe you'll partner with the Spirit in something big and powerful like healing someone who has been ill for decades or something less dramatic like performing a small act of kindness for a stranger. But if you'll join in on what the Father is doing, the love and power of the kingdom will be released, and the world will become a better place because of it.

We've been created to experience the same intimate relationship Jesus shared with his Father:

Anyone who loves me will obey my teaching. My Father will love them and we will come to them and make our home with them. (John 14:23)

Like Jesus, we'll be able to hear the Father's thoughts, speak his words, and do his works. Our task is to train ourselves to be alert to the Father at work around us. I'm not saying this will be easy.

It will take faith to believe that God is actually at work around you in the ordinary, unspectacular routines of your life at home, at school, in your neighborhood, and in your workplace.

The next step is up to you. You'll have to go for it. You can start by praying:

Lord, I want to live this kind of life, so I offer myself up to you this coming week. I ask you to guide my steps. I will do my best to keep my eyes and ears open to see what you are doing and to hear your instructions. I ask for faith to respond with confidence-- offering to pray for whomever you bring my way and to do whatever act of kindness you ask me to perform. Let your kingdom come! Amen.

Reflection and Action

1. Mike describes Jesus' way of doing ministry as "in-the-moment ministry." In your own words, describe what this means.

2. How can we learn to see the work of God around us? What should we be looking for?

3. If we go about life assuming that God is *always* at work around us, how does this change the way that we live? What's different about this perspective than how you have operated previously?

4. As you pray the prayer Mike provides at the end of this chapter, what would happen if God responded to that prayer? What would your life look like? How would you live differently? What would you begin doing?

8 IN STEP WITH THE SPIRIT

The issue of control

If we're going to relate in a healthy, helpful way to the Holy Spirit, we're going to have to hand over control to him, and for many Christians this is easier said than done. For some it brings up all sorts of fears: "If I hand over management of my life to the Spirit I'm going to become some kind of religious robot... a weird fanatic... he'll make me take a vow of poverty or, worse, a vow of celibacy!" Of course this could be true, but it's not all that likely.

What does a healthy relationship with the Spirit look like? Paul described it this way:

16 So I say, walk by the Spirit, and you will not gratify the desires of the flesh. 17 For the flesh desires what is contrary to the Spirit, and the Spirit what is contrary to the flesh. They are in conflict with each other, so that you are not to do whatever you want. 18 But if you are led by the Spirit, you are not under the law. 19 The acts of the flesh are obvious: sexual immorality, impurity and debauchery; 20 idolatry and witchcraft; hatred, discord, jealousy, fits of rage, selfish ambition, dissensions, factions 21 and envy; drunkenness, orgies, and the like. I warn you, as I did before, that those who live like this will not inherit the kingdom of God. 22 But the fruit of the Spirit is love, joy peace, forbearance, kindness, goodness, faithfulness 23 gentleness and self-control. Against such things there is no law. 24 Those who belong to Christ Jesus have crucified the flesh with its passions and desires. 25 Since we live by the Spirit, let us keep in step with the Spirit. 26 Let us not become conceited, provoking and envying each other. (Galatians 5:16-26)

Paul is describing an internal struggle for control between two opposing forces —the flesh and Spirit – with two radically different results-- one dehumanizing and destructive, the other life-giving and fruitful.

Fruitfulness comes from what Paul refers to as *keeping in step* with the Spirit. Think of ballroom dancing. It's all about trust, cooperation, and paying attention. Any inattentiveness, resistance, conflict or power struggle ruins the dance.

The Dance

When I ponder the mystery of the Godhead and the amazing relational chemistry that exists between the Father, Son and Holy Spirit I let my imagination run free and envision an eternal, festive, life-giving dance of love, with lots of harmonious spinning and whirling, emanating life. God brings the cosmos into existence, filling and sustaining everything with the dynamic "movements" of love between the persons of the Trinity. *"For from him and through him and to him are all things."* (Ro. 11:36; see also Acts 17:28) I believe this "dance" is essential, especially for human flourishing as exhibited in the life of Jesus of Nazareth in the gospels (Luke 2:52).

This is the dance Jesus engaged in as seen in the gospels. Jesus' life on earth was lived in total submission to the dance. Everything he did--teaching, healing, casting out demons, calming storms, even dying on the cross and rising from dead-- he did in perfect step with his Father in the power of the Spirit.

You and I have been invited into this dance:

19 Soon the world will no longer see me, but you will see me. Since I live, you also will live. 20 When I am raised to life again, you will know that I am in my Father, and you are in me, and I am in you. 21 Those who accept my commandments and obey them are the ones who love me. And because they love me, my Father will love them. And I will lov e them and reveal myself to each of them." (John 14:19-21)

The triune God wants us to be his dance partners. In this dance, the Spirit leads. We relinquish control and follow, just the way Jesus did. When we cooperate and stay in step, it results in the beautiful movement of abundant life Jesus promised-- the life Jesus himself lived. But the problem is that the sinful pull toward autonomy cripples us; we have two left feet. We need the Spirit to *teach* us how to dance.

Sin has made us control freaks. Relinquishing control doesn't come easy, and what often results is a *power struggle* like the ugly mess that took place in eighth grade between Harvey Press and me.

Every Friday we took a break from Phys Ed and had social dancing instead. We'd learn how to do dances like the waltz, foxtrot, Lindy hop and cha-cha. The boys and girls would line up in alphabetical order and pair off as partners. The problem was that there were always more boys than girls. By the time it got to Harvey and me there were no girls left, and we were left to pair off with each other. Two fourteen-year-old boys locked in a battle over who would lead the dance. It was a matter of honor. A life and death struggle over control! Let's just say what ended up happening was more WrestleMania than Dancing with The Stars. It wasn't pretty. Of course, we'd end-up getting kicked out of the class and sent to the principal's office.

I can think of at least four ways you can mess up the dance. The first way is by *ignorance*. For many Christians the Holy Spirit is a stranger because they've received little or no instruction about who he is and how he works. They're functionally disconnected from the lead dance partner. Get to know God's Word. Study it and pray it, and you'll get to know the Holy Spirit and his dance steps.

The second way to mess up the dance is by holding onto willful, continued sin in your life and refusing to cooperate with the Spirit. As a result, it becomes difficult, if not impossible, to enjoy his presence and power. This is collaborating with the enemy, and it grieves the Spirit. Paul wrote:

And do not grieve the Holy Spirit of God, with whom you were sealed for the day of redemption. (Ephesians 4:30)

The only way to get back in step with the Spirit is to confess your sin, obey, and let him take the lead in the dance.

The third way to mess up is by letting fear keep you from surrendering to the Spirit's leadership. When Paul writes, "...be filled by the Spirit" (Ephesians 5:18), he's referring to the issue of surrendering control to the Spirit. The idea of losing control is frightening to many people. They're afraid that if they hand over control to the Spirit he might ask them to do something embarrassing or crazy. They're afraid he might turn them into someone they don't want to be or send them some place they don't want to go. So they "quench" him—they stifle or put out the fire of his work in their lives. They resist his influence and his help.

Paul warns against this, too:

Do not quench the Spirit. (1 Thessalonians 5:19)

The fourth and perhaps the most common way to mess up the dance is through apathy. The Puritan William Law wrote, "Most Christians are just as holy as they intend to be." The truth is, the only thing that can really keep you from enjoying this life-transforming dance with the Spirit is you. The only people who continue to stumble, are the people who simply don't want to dance. They insist on being contrary. They don't want to stay in step with him. They insist on living the Christian life their own way rather than cooperate with the Spirit.

The key to becoming a good ballroom dance partner is trust and cooperation. It's the same with keeping in step with the Spirit. This means learning to pay attention to him and being willing to trust his leadership and follow his directions. This takes plenty of practice, but over time we can learn to dance.

In spite of what you might think, this has more to do with *not* doing than doing! It's more a matter of allowing ourselves to be overtaken than our pursuing him. This is what Paul was getting at when he wrote, "be filled with the Spirit" (Ephesians 5:18). The Greek word translated *filled* here, carries the idea of *control* or *influence*. In other words, Paul is saying, *"Live constantly under the control of the Holy Spirit"*. Being filled with the Spirit is about his getting more of us rather than our getting more of him.

The issue is control. It a matter of *letting go*, which is the opposite of how we control freaks have been programmed. It's like the time I tried water skiing… When I was in college, our couples Sunday school class went to a lake for a day of waterskiing. I had never tried it. But I thought to myself, how hard could it be? It looks easy enough. I would just grab hold of the rope and, when the boat started, I would pull myself up out of the water and stay on top of it. So that's what I did. I waited in the water behind the boat and held the line tight. As the motor revved I could feel my muscles tensing in anticipation. We started to move. I gripped the line tighter, and, with all the strength I could muster, I pulled myself up… big mistake! I was tossed across the lake like a rag doll. I tried again and again to pull myself upright and stay on top of the water. But the more I tried to power my way to standing, the worse it got! Finally, I was so worn out that I could hardly hold the line any longer. I could only float in the water like a piece of driftwood. I was dead tired. I had virtually no strength left, but I managed to give it one last try.

Barely holding the line, I was unable to do anything but lean back and put myself at the mercy of the boat, skis, and water. To my astonishment, I was now skimming across the lake on top of the water! You see, it wasn't until I stopped trying to muscle my way through, that I finally skied. You might say I had to "die" to self-effort and quietly accept the power of the boat and the influence of the water to move me forward and keep me upright.

In much the same way, the more my flesh (me) insists on being in charge and tries to make things happen, the more I refuse to die to self, the more out of sync with God my life becomes! Inevitably, I make a mess of things. If I'm going to keep in step with the Spirit, I have to quietly accept his control rather than insisting on my own way and trying to muscle my way through life. I have to let go and let God do something for me... lead the dance and direct my life.

For instance, there have been times when the Holy Spirit has wanted me to move when I didn't want to budge. Like when he wouldn't stop pestering me about reconciling with someone who I felt had treated me unjustly and caused me great pain. Quite a bit of time had past without hearing a word of apology from this person but the Spirit was now on my case, prodding me to humble myself and make the first move towards patching things up. I dug my heals in and resisted, thinking, "Doesn't God know I'm the victim here?" But finally, after wrestling in prayer, I gave in and "got in step" with what God was doing. I swallowed my pride, repented of my stubbornness and had a time of forgiveness and healing of our relationship over lunch. Not only was our relationship renewed but to my surprise, it caused me to grow personally in new and unexpected ways.

You see, allowing the Spirit to lead doesn't mean that I do nothing. There *is* something I do. I pray, I pay attention, and I keep saying "yes" to God and quietly accept his control as he leads the dance. Prayer isn't a way I control things: it's the way I participate in the dance and stay in step with the Spirit.

The heavenly music is playing. Do you hear it in your heart? The Spirit is inviting you to step onto the dance floor of life with him. You may have been uninterested, misinformed, too shy, or afraid to dance, but the Spirit is calling nevertheless, "Come..." Will you hand over control to him?

Reflection and Action

1. How would *you* describe a healthy relationship with the Holy Spirit? What would characterize your life and how you make decisions?

2. What prevents you from keeping in step with the Spirit? How would you explain the obstacles you often face? And how do you plan on overcoming those?

3. What do you think about Mike's statement that keeping in step with the Spirit "has more to do with *not doing* than doing"? How does that make you feel? Why?

4. What area of your life do feel the Holy Spirit challenging you to "let go" and let him take more control? What would obedience in that area of life look like for you?

9 ON BEING NATURALLY SUPERNATURAL

You might be thinking, "Naturally supernatural? Haven't we already covered this?" Yes, but now that we've covered so much ground exploring the Spirit-empowered life, I think another look at this important matter might be helpful...

I wrote in an earlier chapter about how I first became a Christian in a Pentecostal chapel service as a resident of Teen Challenge, a Christian drug program in Brooklyn. It was loud, lively and very animated and expressive. It sort of felt like getting pumped-up in the locker room before the big game where the coach gives a big pep talk that revs-up team. Coming from a quiet Roman Catholic background, this Pentecostal style took some getting used to. Particularly strange was the way they prayed. Folks shouted, waved their hands and jumped around! I was told this was what it looked like when the Spirit showed up and did his thing.

Lively and crazy

At first, this boisterousness didn't matter to me. I was desperate for whatever contact with the Spirit I could get, and if it meant getting a little loud and weird, so be it. And you know what, God did meet me and began changing my life. But as time went on I grew more and more uncomfortable with what seemed to be showy, strange and, at times, manipulative behavior. I loved Jesus and the people in the church, but I didn't like the package. It wasn't me. Eventually, I became gun shy and avoided the Spirit and anything that might smack of weirdness – like speaking in tongues, prophesying, or casting out demons – as much as possible. However, keeping the Spirit at arms distance may have been more comfortable, but along the way I lost something...

50

I could be myself

When I ran into John Wimber, the founder of the Vineyard movement, I saw something different. John wasn't interested in putting on a show and wowing the crowd. There was no hype, weirdness or manipulation. When he ministered, he was relaxed, comfortable, real. I was impressed with how he remained normal even while worshiping and praying. He called it being *"naturally supernatural"*.

John was the same person during ministry time that he was during dinnertime! I learned that I didn't have to put on some spiritual persona, change the tone of my voice when I prayed, or get dramatic or frenzied in order for the Spirit to move. And the most significant and liberating discovery was that I could just be myself and God would still show up! Boy, did that take the pressure off! I could respond to the promptings of the Spirit in my own, authentic way. That was huge! My response to this freedom was, *"I can do that! I want to do that!"* I was off and running "doing the stuff" of the kingdom, and I haven't stopped since…

This is big!

The implications of being *naturally supernaturally* are huge:

- It means everyone gets to participate in what God is doing in the world today. You can be uniquely yourself, and God can still use you.

- It relieves the pressure to perform. You can act normal, and God will still show up.

- It opens up ministry opportunities out in the marketplace of life, at home, at work, in your neighborhood, not just inside the church.

- Outsiders don't feel threatened or put-off by the Spirit because there's no weirdness, hype or manipulation. Receptivity increases dramatically.

- And finally, being *naturally supernatural* paves the way for people to actually experience God's loving and healing presence in a way that feels neither threatening nor embarrassing.

Breaking the negative stereotype

In our secular world, where often a person's only reference for the supernatural is Hollywood fantasy and reality TV weirdness, the comfort of God's Spirit being exhibited in *naturally supernatural* ways breaks the negative stereotype of what Christians are like and is for many the start of a faith journey of their own. Being naturally supernatural allows us to be wonderfully subversive the way Jesus was.

When you're able to be natural and comfortable to be around, people let down their guard and open up to you, to God, and to new possibilities for their lives. It allows us to partner with God and be useful to the kingdom in all the places "religious" people are mostly useless - out in the marketplace of life. Being naturally supernatural opens a way for us to have a positive, life-giving impact among our non-religious relatives, friends, and neighbors, in our workplaces, schools, and the places we gather to relax and have fun...

When we conduct ourselves in naturally supernatural ways, good things seem to happen. Those around us experience the presence and power of God right where they are in non-threatening ways that leave them with a good taste in their mouths-- and wanting more. What's more, we get to impact the most unlikely people – folks that are presently uninterested in Christianity. And when we live our lives as *cooperative friends of Jesus, creatively doing good for the sake of others by the power of the Holy Spirit*, that brings *us* joy in any number of new, refreshing and exciting ways.

It's a lifestyle
Jesus was the prototypical, naturally supernatural human. He brought the kingdom of God up-close-and-personal to ordinary, everyday folk simply by being approachable and involved in the affairs of their normal, everyday lives.

So what does a naturally supernatural lifestyle look like? When most people think of being used by God, they think of something demanding and difficult, something otherworldly and strange-- way out of their league and comfort zone. But that's not it at all. Actually, it looks like YOU when you're at your best-- relaxed, not self-conscious, being yourself, loving God, and spontaneously and creatively keeping in step with what the Spirit is doing-- being the fully empowered human being God created you to be.

Being naturally supernatural is about being alert to God's Spirit showing up in the midst of your daily routines and using you to help those around you. For my wife and me, being naturally supernatural has been mostly wrapped in the unspectacular and ordinary. It's meant simply being good neighbors. That's led to being invited into people's lives, which has often opened a natural, relaxed way of sharing our faith stories with them and opened their eyes and hearts to a God who is present and has power to be a difference-maker in their lives.

Over the years, being naturally supernatural has led to many of our neighbors becoming comfortable talking about God and even asking for prayer.

A number have found faith in Jesus. You might say that the most powerful naturally supernatural thing we've done is offer friendship, hospitality, and prayer to our neighbors. This makes perfect sense because the Holy Spirit is friendly!

If you want to have a naturally supernatural impact on people, be friendly. It opens all kinds of doors for ministry.

So how do you become naturally supernatural? It's all about being open, alert, and available to the Holy Spirit. It's a matter of responding obediently to his ofttimes unexpected, even inconvenient whispers, nudges, and promptings. It's letting him custom-fit you with an *incarnational lifestyle* that looks like Jesus if he were you--a lifestyle that shows others around you what God is like by living like Jesus and doing the things he did. It's being a good neighbor the way Jesus would be a neighbor if he were you. Being a nurturing and encouraging grandparent the way Jesus would be a grandparent. Being an excellent teacher the way Jesus would be a teacher if he taught your students. Being a competent and responsible custodian the way Jesus would be a custodian if he did your job. It can't be done in isolation. It's about living connected to Jesus while connecting with your neighbors, co-workers, and classmates--which means you'll have to get out of your cocoon and socialize and make friends. It also means living with a *purpose* – with an awareness that, as a follower of Jesus, you've been invited to participate in his mission of loving people and making the world around you a better place.

One last thing: to keep your naturally supernatural lifestyle fresh and ongoing, you'll have to keep giving away what God has freely given to you-- *his love!*

Being naturally supernatural isn't a self-improvement program or a path to enjoying private spiritual experiences. It's about doing good for the sake of others by the power of the Holy Spirit, a lifestyle of Spirit-empowered friendship and service.

Reflection and Action

1. Explain in your own words what it means to be "naturally supernatural" and how is this different than "lively and crazy"?

2. Why do you think living out of your authentic self is such an important aspect of partnering with the Holy Spirit for the purpose of kingdom ministry?

3. Who is the most "naturally supernatural" person you know and what have you learned from them?

4. Mike describes "naturally supernatural" as being "about doing good for the sake of others by the power of the Holy Spirit." Why is this an important foundation to keep in mind?

5. What actions are you taking too be "a cooperative friend of Jesus"?

10 MIDWIFING

A lot of people, Christians and non-Christians alike, have been turned off and even damaged by charismatic-type ministry gone wrong—whether it was insensitive, manipulative, lacking integrity or just plain weird. In most cases it's the *package* that's the problem - the way the person doing the ministry is acting. People are left with such a bad taste in their mouths that they end up throwing the baby out with the bath water, not wanting to have anything whatsoever to do with things of the Spirit, or, worse, giving up on church or Christianity altogether.

As followers of Jesus, our challenge is to be like him and take his ministry into the marketplace of life where a hurting yet skeptical world awaits. But today, more than ever, the messenger *is* the message. The sort of people we are--how we carry ourselves, how we treat others, how we do ministry-- can speak louder than anything we have to say. We can be attractive representatives of Jesus' mission or turn-offs: "I like what you're telling me about Jesus, but if it means becoming like you, I don't want any part of it!" The package that kingdom ministry comes in is extremely important. It can be the difference between people being open and receptive or slamming the door in our faces. When we're *naturally supernatural,* people can become aware of the reality of God's love, power and care for them in relaxed, normal ways that are nonthreatening and engaging.

A way of praying
The first time I ever heard "midwife" and "prayer" used in the same sentence was in a healing seminar conducted by John Wimber, the founder of the Vineyard. He was talking about how people are often treated inconsiderately in charismatic ministry-- like objects rather than people—with the result that more harm is often done than good.

People who experience this kind of treatment may feel embarrassed, used, and even violated. Some victims of this type of abuse give up on Christianity and become its biggest critics. Wimber pointed out that Jesus didn't minister to people that way. He treated them with love, dignity, and respect. Jesus was attentive and thoughtful. Every person he ministered to felt valued and cared for. As Wimber put it: "Jesus was like a *midwife of the Holy Spirit."* The term *Spirit midwife* captures well both the intention and the feel of what it means to minister in a naturally supernatural manner. That image has stuck with me and helped launch me into a healing-prayer ministry modeled on Jesus' loving and attentive partnership with the Spirit.

What midwives do

Midwives are remarkable. They offer a special kind of care to mothers giving birth by entering into a relationship with a singular purpose: to make sure both mom and baby are comfortable and safe so that the delivery goes well. I actually got to see a midwife in action during the birth of one of my grandchildren (although I excused myself when it got down to the finish line). As I watched her quietly and skillfully go about her business, Wimber's Spirit midwife image came alive. Two things in particular stood out to me: the midwife's calming effect on the the proceedings and her "coaching" of the mother through the birth. She set a friendly, relaxed tone that put the mother at ease during what is an extremely strange and stressful experience. She remained calm under pressure as she provided support and reassurance. She was attentive, patient, and non-intrusive--never trying to force anything to happen in the course of the birth process.

You could tell she was in her element. She was knowledgeable and at home with the whole business of childbirth which made an arduous and unfamiliar experience for the mother easier. The midwife didn't try to control the situation but paid close attention to what was going on. Nothing got past her. There wasn't a contraction, the slightest increase in the mother's or baby's heart rate, any hiccup that she wasn't on top of as she coached, comforted, explained or adjusted so that the birth could move on.

Spirit midwives

The skill set and posture of a midwife translate particularly well into naturally supernatural-style prayer ministry as we try to keep in step with what the Spirit is doing. Jesus said, "My Father is always at work." (John 5:17) Our Creator and Redeemer God continues to work through his Spirit, giving birth to salvation, healing, and new creation in people's lives.

God...wants all people to be saved and come to a knowledge of the truth (1 Timothy 2:3-4)

The Father is at work, all the time, in the lives of people all around you-- in your family, your workplace, your neighborhood, your city or town, outside your church, among the most unlikely people in the most unlikely places. A Spirit midwife's role is not to do the Spirit's work but to be alert, pay attention, recognize where the Spirit is working in others' lives, and assist in the delivery.

Spirit-midwives have one objective: to make sure the delivery goes well. They want to make sure that the person or persons the Spirit is ministering to receive everything the Lord wants to give birth to in their lives. And like all good midwives, they set a tone that makes what can otherwise be difficult— even scary-- as safe and comfortable as possible.

Receiving prayer, like giving birth, is a strange and mysterious experience. Prayer ministry can also be intimate and personal. People make themselves vulnerable when they receive prayer. They often put themselves in the hands of a minister they don't know that well. They need to be protected from embarrassment and treated with care and respect. Midwives are mindful of this.

Let me say a word about the laying on of hands – the practice of placing a hand on the person receiving prayer and imparting the Lord's healing power. Jesus often healed people by touching them (Matt. 8:15) but not always. He used many patterns and methods in healing such as a word or command (Luke 5:24), someone touching him (Luke 8:44), using spittle or mud (Mark 7:33). While laying hands is often an effective way to pray, the Spirit midwife understands that this may not always be appropriate. Touch conveys different things to different people depending on their make-up and experiences. For one, touch may communicate care and affection. To another that same touch can be threatening. Knowing this, a midwife always asks permission to lay hands on the person being prayed for.

The midwife's most important tool: prayer

Spirit midwives don't manipulate or force things to happen. They pray. Prayer is their stock-in-trade. Midwiving is Spirit-directed care dispensed through prayer.

A Spirit midwife's view of prayer is that it doesn't get us what we want but what God wants. Eugene Peterson says that prayer is never the first word-- it's always the "second word". God always has the first word. Holy Spirit midwives pay attention and listen carefully to what the Spirit is saying. Prayer becomes "answering speech." It's, "Lord, let me do what you're (already) blessing" rather than "Bless what I'm doing."

Spirit midwives begin in a place of God-consciousness, not self-consciousness. They first ask, "Father, what are you doing?... Show me what to do... Tell me how to pray..." Then they do it.

Spirit midwives hand control over to the Spirit, inviting him to do his work while they do their job of maintaining a safe atmosphere that's conducive to healing. They pay close attention and listen carefully. They give one ear to the person being prayed for and their best ear to God so they can pray Spirit-guided prayers. They focus on helping those receiving prayer to relax, cooperate with what the Spirit is doing, and receive everything God wants to give birth in them.

What about the role of faith in healing ministry? It's clear Jesus was more able to heal in the presence of faith in him and in his power to heal (Matthew 9:2; Mark 5:34). He sometimes healed when he alone believed, but he was clearly limited by a negative faith atmosphere (Mark 6:5-6). It seems clear that faith is necessary in some way in healing ministry, whether present in the person praying, the person receiving prayer or some third party (Luke 17-20). However, our faith never controls God. Midwives never control, the Spirit does. We cannot by our faith force God to do what we want, when we want it.

How does someone become a midwife of the Holy Spirit? Like many things in Holy Spirit ministry, it's more caught than taught, and this happens most naturally when an experienced Spirit midwife takes a beginner under his or her wing and, as with an apprentice, passes on these prayer skills through a process that involves modeling, impartation, coaching, and plenty of practice.

Reflection and Action

1. Do you agree that in today's world, "the messenger is the message"? Why is the "package" such an important part of kingdom ministry? Why is the image of a midwife helpful?

2. Were you in the position of receiving ministry or prayer from someone, what would help your experience to remain positive? What characteristics would you want the person praying for you to exhibit? How would you want to be treated?

3. Have you ever helped someone experience the presence of God by ministering to them? What seemed to work? Were there things you said or did that you now think you could have done differently?

4. Who are some people that you can learn "Spirit midwifing" from? How can you learn this practice and move forward to become more effective at ministering to people?

11 FAMILIARITY, SOAP BUBBLES & TROUT FISHING – HEARING GOD'S VOICE

've often heard the complaint from Christians, "I can't hear God's voice" or "God never speaks to me!" What I think they really mean is that God doesn't speak to them in dramatic fashion, like a thundering voice from heaven or in a spectacular vision. I know God does speak to them, and they can hear him--they just might not be paying attention or don't know what to listen for.

It's a matter of lack of *familiarity*.

A shepherd's voice
There's a direct link between hearing the Lord's voice and keeping company with him. Jesus used the image of a shepherd and his sheep to explain this relationship:

...the sheep listen to his voice. He calls his own sheep by name and leads them out. When he has brought out all his own, he goes on ahead of them, and his sheep follow him because they know his voice. But they will never follow a stranger; in fact, they will run away from him because they do not recognize a stranger's voice... I am the good shepherd; I know my sheep and my sheep know me... My sheep listen to my voice; I know them, and they follow me. (John 10:3-5,14,27)

In the Middle East sheep have incredible personal relationships with each of their shepherds. They spend most of their lives together. Someone else can come into the sheep pen, and the sheep won't go near him, even if he calls their names.

60

They listen for the one voice that matters, the voice they've come to trust. When they hear it, they'll follow.

When Jesus says, "I *know* my sheep and my sheep *know* me," he's not referring to second-hand knowledge or the casual "knowing" of an acquaintance. He's referring to an intimate, growing relationship.

Married couples

It's the knowledge married couples acquire through having shared a lifetime of experiences. After having spent so much time together, they know each other completely, inside and out.

Let's say someone claiming to be my wife leaves a message on my phone saying, "Honey, get the old fish tank ready. I'm bringing home a python I picked up at the pet store." Even if it's a pretty good impersonation, I'd immediately know it's not her. First of all, after forty-six years of marriage, I know my wife's voice. I'm hearing impaired, and yet I can still pick her voice out of a noisy room of people. After all these years, there's instant recognition. I can even tell her mood and the kind of day she's having by the tone of her voice.

I not only know the sound of my wife's voice, I know her – her facial expressions, her moods, the way she thinks, what she likes and doesn't like. I can predict with some accuracy how she would react to most situations. And I know with absolute certainty that my wife is terrified of snakes. So when I check the message, I can quickly tell you, "Yes, that's Char" or "Hold on, my wife would never leave a message like that. This is not my wife. Someone's pulling my leg."

"Just knowing"

My wife and I have become so familiar with each other that we've developed a kind of "automatic knowing" A sort of instant recognition. When asked how it works I just say, "We just know". My answer might exasperate someone who has never experienced this kind of familiarity. But that's the way familiarity works… you just know.

It reminds me of a blog post I once read written by a young lady:

"How do you know when God is speaking to you?" I would often ask my mom this question in my early years of being a Christian. I had no doubt that God indeed spoke to his children, but I wanted to be sure I didn't miss his voice.

My mom would always give me the same answer, 'Baby, you'll know!' At times her answer frustrated me because I wanted a formula for knowing, like A+B=C, so I'd know for sure God was speaking to me. Over the years, as I grew in my Christian walk, I came to understand why she didn't give me a simple formula, there isn't one.

She's right, after all, Jesus simply said, "My sheep recognize my voice and they follow me" (John 10:27).

This is a well-known and beloved passage, but it's also a frustrating one because we want the recipe and Jesus simply says, "You'll know".

My wife and I didn't arrive at the familiarity we share by reading a textbook or following certain steps. We developed it by sharing life together. It's the result of an intimate relationship. When you spend enough time getting to know someone, like the young blogger's mom said, "You just know." I think this is the kind of familiarity Jesus had in mind when he said, "My sheep recognize my voice and they follow me."

Listening impaired

How will you know when it's God speaking and not one of the other voices you hear in your head? It comes down to familiarity, and that comes down to spending time with him. Too often people treat God like a stranger and then complain that he's silent or distant.

The problem is that most of us are not accustomed to listening. We're trained to use our minds to get information, complete assignments, run errands, and carry out tasks. We don't know how to quiet ourselves in God's presence and shift our minds into listening mode. Consequently, many of us have become "listening impaired" and don't hear his voice because he can only reach us when we decelerate and quiet ourselves.

"Be still and know I'm God..." (Psalm 46:10)

Dallas Willard once advised a friend, "Ruthlessly eliminate hurry." We've become a society of "speed addicts." Our world has become noisy and harried. We're too busy and in a rush. Few of us slow down long enough to pay attention to what's going on around us let alone inside us. Most of us are too distracted by our addiction to busyness to invest the time it takes to become familiar with God and hear God's voice when he speaks.

Another time Willard asked a friend the question: "If you had *one word* to describe Jesus what would it be?" Lots of words come to mind: *Powerful... Compassionate... Holy...* Willard's word for Jesus was unexpected. His one word was "relaxed" or "unhurried." Now that's a word few of us would come up with considering all the pressure Jesus was constantly under. In his retelling, Willard's friend admitted, "I wasn't sure I liked that word! It made me nervous. It made me feel itchy!" That's because he was addicted to speed.

Are you a speed addict? You have to slow down and detox. It will take some re-training to learn how to listen and pay attention to things you're not normally used to hearing – things like the whispers, promptings, subtle nudges, spontaneous thoughts and pictures from the Spirit that we fail to notice or dismiss because our addiction to busyness and noise has made us listening impaired.

God's voice or thoughts from God are different than other voices and thoughts we hear in our heads. They don't come through our normal thought processes. For me, they often just seem to suddenly "appear"-- like they've been dropped into my spirit. They also have a different "feel" to them, a weightiness. Two illustrations might help capture what I mean: catching soap bubbles and trout fishing.

Soap bubbles

God usually doesn't shout. He's subtle. He speaks lightly, in a "still, small voice." He whispers. His thoughts, as experienced in our minds, are here one moment and gone the next. What I'm describing as "hearing" can be experienced in a variety of ways, depending on the individual's unique make-up. It might come as an audible inner voice, or a strong thought or impression or feeling. At other times it might be an image in one's mind.

Learning to listen to God is a lot like catching soap bubbles. Soap bubbles float around spontaneously and unforced. You have to be very careful with them: if you try too hard and grab at them, they'll burst. You have to relax and let them come to you. They're very delicate. You have to pay close attention to them before they drift away or disappear. Soap bubbles are beautiful. When they're in your hand they sparkle and shimmer like jewels, but they last only for a brief moment and then they're gone.

To hear God's voice or receive his thoughts in some other form is a lot like catching soap bubbles. This kind of hearing is trans-rational.

It's different than my normal thought process. It's Spirit to spirit communication. You might say it's a heart thing rather than a head thing. Hearing God speak is often unexpected, out of the blue. As with a soap bubble, it's best not to try and grab at it right away with my rational mind. I have to tune into a kind of playful spontaneity and avoid overthinking things, which can get me hung up in doubt.

It's important to mention a word about the work of discernment that goes along with hearing God's voice. Not every voice we hear in our head or outstanding thought that pops up in our mind or striking image or intense feeling or impression that stirs us, is God. Our own desires, emotions and fears are very strong and compelling. They can be mistaken for the voice of God. So care should be taken to make sure that any decisions or actions taken on the basis of what you might think is God speaking to you should be accompanied by the use of some sound judgement. You can ask yourself questions like, "Is this in line with the Bible?" and "Is this something Jesus would say or do?" and "Will this bear loving and edifying fruit?" When possible seek the counsel of others. Preferably those wiser than yourself. Of course not every "word" is as consequential as others and requires as much deliberation and reflection. The more familiar we become with our Good Shepherd, the more discernment can be done in the moment.

It seems that I 'catch' God's whispers most easily when my mind is at rest-- when it's not working that hard. So I have to teach myself to slow down, quiet myself, and just be in God's presence. I have to get used to listening for and paying attention to the little, light, soap bubbly things that float into my spirit. I need to learn not to dismiss them as just my imagination, but consider that they might be from God, exercise discernment and pray into them instead.

Trout fishing
The Spirit's voice is different from the normal course your mind takes: if you're not familiar with it and tuned into its spontaneity, you'll mistake it for something else ("Oh that's just my imagination...") or miss it altogether. That brings us to a second illustration: Trout fishing.

A friend got me to go trout fishing with him. I had never tried it so I agreed to give it a go. My friend showed me what to do: First, bait your hook, and then cast the line into the stream and begin slowly reeling it in with the hope that some hungry trout would grab it for lunch.

Simply cast and reel: it seemed simple enough. I repeated it over and over. Cast, reel... Cast, reel... Every so often I'd feel a tug on my line. My rod would bend and my heart would jump with excitement as I reeled in my line only to discover-- to my disappointment-- that I had hooked a clump of weeds or a piece of driftwood. The tug felt so real-- like I imagined a real trout would feel on the end of my line. This kept on happening: Cast...reel... tug... adrenaline... reel... fooled again... disappointment, until... I hooked my first real trout! It felt different than a dead clump of weeds. It felt alive! After experiencing a few more catches, I wasn't so easily fooled because I now knew the feel of the real thing. And after a few more fishing outings under my belt, I was familiar enough with the feel of a live fish on the end of my line that I didn't have to wonder if my "catch" was a fish or just some weeds. I just knew it.

Early on, before I had ever experienced a prophetic word or word of knowledge, I'd wonder how it worked. What was it like to receive a word from God? And how could I tell when it was God speaking from all the other voices and thoughts that were playing in my head? It was all a bit confusing, and I got fooled a lot until I experienced my first word of knowledge. It was different! It had a different feel. It had "weight" to it-- a certain sense of importance and authority that set it apart from my ordinary thoughts. It came with a little rush of excitement that resonated in my inner being as right and true. As time went on and I spent more time with Jesus, I became more and more familiar with him and his voice, to the point where now this is almost second nature to me. Like a sheep with his shepherd, I "just know" when it's his Spirit speaking to me.

Moving forward
So for those of you who are new to all this, be patient with yourself. This sort of discernment doesn't happen overnight. It takes time and practice to develop. The best way to start is to spend quiet time with Jesus each day. Do your best to slow down and relax in his presence and just be. Fight the urge to fill the silence with talk. Just be still and listen. Start out doing this for ten minutes a day and see what happens. Once you get more comfortable doing nothing, you might add meditating on a passage of Scripture and letting it speak to you. Over time, if you stick with it and are consistent, your ability to recognize your Shepherd's voice will sharpen and become second nature. You, too, will "just know" and be able to follow were he's leading you.

It will be challenging at first, but your time alone with Jesus will become more and more important and enjoyable. Ten minutes will become fifteen minutes and, before you know it, twenty, thirty minutes a day...

Ruth Haley Barton wrote: "The capacity to recognize the voice of God arises out of friendship with God that is sustained through prayer... silent... listening... and attentiveness to all that is going on outside us, inside us and between us and God. Through practice and experience we become familiar with the tone of God's voice, the content of his communications with us and his unique, individual way of addressing us."

Again a word of caution here: strong emotions or desires can sound or feel like God speaking. Tuning into the spontaneous inner flow of God's thoughts, impressions, and visions may seem pretty risky. But there are some guidelines we can follow. They dovetail with my earlier suggestions about discernment: First, all major decisions that come as a result of hearing from God should be checked out with the Bible. Second, it's also very important for your growth and safety that you are part of a solid community of believers who can offer perspective and objectivity in what you are hearing from God. Third, when it comes to major decision making, I suggest that before acting on any thoughts, impressions, or visions you seek the counsel of other trusted members of your community-- especially pastoral leadership-- and have your sense confirmed.

Reflection and Action

1. Do you think it's possible that God's been speaking to you more than you realize? Explain your reason for believing this.

2. If you believe God has spoken to you in the past, describe what his voice sounds like. What are the various ways that God speaks to people?

3. Mike points us to John 10:27, where Jesus says his sheep know his voice. How does this concept strike you and what would you say keeps us from recognizing God's voice?

4. What do you find most challenging about "tuning into spontaneity" and the idea of handling "soap bubbles"? What changes in your lifestyle might help?

5. Many people assume that God only speaks to "holy people" or "church leaders," yet the Bible teaches us that all of Jesus' followers can learn to recognize his voice. What do you need to do in order to become a better listener?

6. In order to become more discerning, how can followers of Jesus learn to differentiate between the voice of God, their own emotions, or lies from the enemy?

12 TRAINING WHEELS - FIVE STEP PRAYER MODEL

Have you ever been in that tense, uneasy position of praying in a public place for someone - maybe a friend in a café over a cup of coffee? Your heart's pounding. The adrenaline is pumping. A sense of trepidation comes over you as you fight to keep your mind from going blank. The only thought you do have is, "I just know I'm gonna blow this." So you shut your eyes and awkwardly start praying the first thing you think would be helpful that pops into your mind-- rushing through it as if the room is on fire. And when it's over, there's relief and a little weirdness hanging in the air. It's in moments like this that I bet you wished you had some help to guide you.

Jesus-style prayer

How did Jesus manage to pray under the most pressurized, distracting and unfriendly conditions? Did he have help? Did he follow some blueprint that kept him focused and on track? A casual look at the gospels doesn't reveal any discernable pattern: Jesus prayed all sorts of ways. He prayed both publicly and privately. He used commands and touch. He even used spit and mud! It seems his prayers were tailor-made for whatever the situation called for. But when pressed to explain how he did what he did, Jesus said that he paid attention to his Father and simply followed what he was doing.

...the Son can do nothing by himself; he can do only what he sees his Father doing, because whatever the Father does the Son also does. (John 5:19).

He used a *watch, listen, ask* and *obey* method. He later told his disciples that they could learn to do the same thing.

Whoever believes in me will do the works I have been doing... (John 14:7)

John Wimber taught a naturally supernatural way of praying based on Christ's watch, listen, ask and obey approach. He called it the Five-Step Prayer Model, and it's not just for the superstars and the extremely gifted. With practice any believer can learn to use it in order to partner with the Father's work by the Spirit.

Training wheels

The model isn't magic-- it's just a helpful tool. Think of the prayer model as training wheels that steady the person doing the praying by helping him or her gain the confidence and focus needed to stay on track and follow the Spirit. It follows Jesus' watch, listen, ask, and obey approach. Each step answers a question that helps us "see what the Father's doing" and pay attention to the Holy Spirit. It helps us determine the condition of the person being prayed for and what God is up to in the moment: What's the problem? What's the Father doing? How should I pray? Is anything happening? When should we stop praying?

The five steps are explained in detail in Wimber's book *Power Healing* and in a number of other Vineyard resources, so I'm just going to mention them briefly and add a few comments and tips I've found helpful...

Working the model

The first step is *The Interview*. This answers the question: "What's the problem or need I'm praying for?" The interview not only gives us a place to begin, but it also sets the tone and direction for what has the potential to become a significant divine encounter, so being friendly, paying attention, and listening are essential.

Showing empathy, warmth, and respect helps cut through any nervousness or reservations on the part of the the person being prayed for so that he or she can relax and receive. Even if nothing else happens in the prayer time, the person has been shown kindness and experienced loving care, which is beneficial in and of itself.

Listening carefully to the person being prayed for is important, but even more important is listening to God. Francis MacNutt offers this bit of advice: "Give one ear to the person and your best ear to God." As the person shares with you, stay alert.

The Spirit may highlight something being said for you to focus on, or he may give you a word of knowledge that gives you insight into what to pray for and how to pray.

This leads to the second step, called *Diagnosis and Prayer Selection*. Based on the interview, I decide what to pray for and how to pray for it. I pray differently for a physical problem than I would for an emotional wound or for addressing demonic activity. Each root cause requires a different approach.

Furthermore, presenting problems can be symptoms of a deeper problem. For example, things like stomach ulcers and migraine headaches can be caused by stress. The ulcer or migraine may not go away by simply praying for the symptom—it may be that the stress must be dealt with first, possibly through forgiveness or emotional healing. Once when praying for a little old lady who was suffering from a disorder that made digesting her meals very difficult, I noticed she began acting very strangely when I invited the Holy Spirit. I sensed that demonic activity might be the underlying cause her physical problem. When I addressed the spirit, the lady began to groan and then passed out! I prayed a prayer of deliverance and watched has she lay there in peace. A few minutes later she awoke with a bright, clear look in her eyes. That later, after our dinner break, she reported that for the first time in years she was able to eat a full meal without any problems.

Discerning root causes from symptoms sounds complicated, but armed with the information I have--from listening to the person and listening to the Spirit-- I step out in faith, do my best to make at least an initial diagnosis, pick a prayer, and go for it, knowing that the Spirit may change my approach as we move on in the prayer time.

The third step is *Prayer Engagement*. That simply means start praying. Before beginning, I "dial down," quieting my inner noise, slowing down, and taking a few deep breaths so I can sense the promptings of the Spirit. When I've done that, I begin praying by inviting the Holy Spirit. "Come, Holy Spirit." I don't raise my voice. I pray in a normal conversational tone. I also keep my eyes open. This is difficult for many people who are used to closing their eyes when they pray, but you can train yourself to do this because it's important: much of the way I can tell what the Spirit is doing and follow his lead is based on what I observe, and using all of the senses available to me helps me do this. People respond to the presence of the Spirit in a variety of ways. I look for physical or emotional signs of his activity so I can bless what he's doing.

I don't know why, but when I keep my eyes open, I seem to be able to hear the whispers of the Spirit more clearly as well.

I continue to watch, listen, and pray as I sense the Spirit directing me. In the case of physical or demonic problems, I use prayers of command, addressing the condition in a personal way. "Headache, be gone!"... "Cancer cells, I curse you in Jesus name!"... "In the name of Jesus, infection, be gone!"...This is weird, but Jesus commanded storms to quiet down and fevers to be gone, so I do it, too. It seems I tap into Christ's authority and power in a greater way when I pray this way, so I keep doing it.

The fourth step is the scariest. Many try to avoid it. I call it *Checking In.* Having invited the Spirit and prayed, it's now time to ask the person to report on what's going on. Has anything happened or changed?

Prayer ministry is risky. It takes faith. "What if nothing happens?"... No one wants to find out they've failed! And this is why we're sometimes afraid to ask. It's easier (and safer) to simply say "Amen" and call it a day. But how will I know if my prayer is having any effect if I don't ask? What if the Spirit is at work in some hidden way in the person that might lead to something big if I were to continue praying? I wouldn't know if I didn't ask. Feedback on what prayers and words were helpful and which ones weren't can help us grow in learning to discern God's voice and express what we hear to others. And if something significant has happened or is happening, can be very encouraging and a big boost to our faith.

What's the worst that can happen if nothing happens? At the very least, the person I prayer for felt cared for and comforted. He or she experienced God's loving kindness. If that's the worst that can happen, I'll risk asking the question in case there's more than meets the eye that can encourage me and help me grow in praying for others in the future.

It's important not to rush your prayer even if you're nervous. Fight it. Be patient. I've found that the Holy Spirit doesn't seem to be in a hurry, so I've had to learn to take my time. I may have to pray another time after checking in. So I just repeat the process again. I believe one of the reasons we don't see more happen when we pray for the sick is that we stop too soon.

But there is a time to stop praying. How can you tell? The Spirit lifts, and you or the person being prayed for can tell. In most cases, if the person you're praying for is done, you're done. Don't push it.

Communicate a willingness to pray for them again, but don't force them to get back into it if they're ready to move on. That can be weird and annoying. That brings us to the final step, *Post-Prayer Direction*. This step answers the question: "What should this person do next?"

This can go in lots of directions depending on the situation and whether the person was healed or not, so continue to be open to the Spirit's direction. While I don't encourage giving advice, the Spirit may give you a word of support or wisdom. It can be an encouragement to get more prayer or to attend a home group in order to deepen one's relationship with God.

Two things we don't do: If nothing has happened, we don't blame it on a lack of faith. Although faith does play an important part, healing prayer is a complex and mysterious matter. It's best to be honest about that, admit you don't know why healing doesn't happen sometimes, and advocate for more prayer. The other thing we never do is tell someone to stop taking their medication, even if it appears healing has taken place. If this is the case (hooray!), tell the person who has been healed to be checked by their physician for confirmation before discontinuing medications and such. This is not a lack of faith, it's a matter of being prudent and caring for people well.

A final word
There are a couple of drawbacks with using a prayer model that you should keep in mind. First, it's worth mentioning again that with any pattern that makes you more effective there's a danger of attaching magical powers to it. The prayer model is not a formula for insuring success. It's just a simple way to get started and stay on track with what God's doing. It helps remove the fear of praying for others and limits the weirdness in what can be a rather mysterious encounter. The second drawback is that it can become mechanical and legalistic. This model is not written in stone. It's not sacred. It doesn't have to be followed to the letter. As you practice and become more comfortable with it, you may discover a pattern of watching, listening, and obeying that suits you better. But until you do, keep the five-step prayer model handy when the Lord calls on you to pray for someone at church or in your small group or for those unexpected moments in the marketplace of life when God shows up and wants to use your prayers to reveal his love and power to those he brings your way.

Reflection and Action

1. What would you say are the top three reasons that keep people from offering to pray for people? How can you overcome those obstacles?

2. Earlier we discussed being "Naturally Supernatural." How will the Five-Step Prayer Model help you remain authentic, loving, and effective as you take steps of faith and risk offering to pray for people?

3. Does "checking in," the fourth step, feel unspiritual? Why or why not? In your opinion, what makes this step an important part of the process?

4. If you are in a group, take some time to ask each other what each of you need prayer for. Now take time to practice the Five-Step Prayer Model on each other. What did you learn? How can you improve? What can you celebrate as genuine evidence of God's presence and power?

5. What can you do to keep this prayer model from becoming a stale routine?

13 THE MIRACLE OF PENTECOST

The miracle of Pentecost was a miracle of hearing. It was a miracle of crossing social barriers and entering the world of others-- a miracle of communication by the power of God's Spirit, which is as much a miracle today as it was back in the first century.

When the Feast of Pentecost came, they were all together in one place. Without warning there was a sound like a strong wind, gale force—no one could tell where it came from. It filled the whole building. Then, like a wildfire, the Holy Spirit spread through their ranks, and they started speaking in a number of different languages as the Spirit prompted them.

There were many Jews staying in Jerusalem just then, devout pilgrims from all over the world. When they heard the sound, they came on the run. Then when they heard, one after another, their own mother tongues being spoken, they were thunderstruck. They couldn't for the life of them figure out what was going on, and kept saying, "Aren't these all Galileans? How come we're hearing them talk in our various mother tongues?

Parthians, Medes, and Elamites; Visitors from Mesopotamia, Judea, and Cappadocia, Pontus and Asia, Phrygia and Pamphylia, Egypt and the parts of Libya belonging to Cyrene; Immigrants from Rome, both Jews and proselytes; Even Cretans and Arabs!

"They're speaking our languages, describing God's mighty works!" (Acts 2:1-11 MSG)

I grew up in a public housing project in the Bronx. The residents were predominantly second generation immigrants, working class Irish, Italian, black and Puerto Rican families. We all spoke English and managed, for the most part, to get along. Then a family moved in across the hall from us.

They were Hispanic but not Puerto Rican. We didn't know where they were from and never bothered to find out because they didn't speak English, and we didn't speak Spanish. We remained a mystery to one another. The closest we got to connecting was an occasional polite nod on our way out of the building. Although we lived just a few yards from each other, there was a barrier we never got past. Without a common language we remained separated by a wall of uneasiness and suspicion.

A recent report I came across asked the question: "Where in the world is the largest number of different languages spoken?"

The report went on to say that conventional wisdom, and even a number of experienced linguists, would probably offer New Guinea as the answer. But there's another place in the world that now surpasses that island when it comes to diverse languages. According to recent linguistic studies, the five boroughs of New York City are reckoned to be home to speakers of around 800 languages!

The world in all its diversity is no longer on the other side of the globe. The whole wide world is on our doorstep. This makes some people nervous and unhappy. They see this as a threat to their way of seeing the world… A threat to their own culture… A threat to their faith… So some of them try to bar admission to "their" society. They try to erect walls to keep difference out-- sort of like how my family and I treated our neighbors across the hall who spoke a different language than we did.

This attitude runs exactly opposite to the expansive and inclusive message of the gospel of Jesus Christ. People from language groups scattered throughout the ancient world were together on the day the church was born in a world both as diverse and divided as our own.

The story of the church's birth in Acts begins in the middle of a noisy mixture of different languages. A holiday crowd filled the streets of Jerusalem with people from all over-- from Parthia and Mesopotamia in the north and east, to the island of Crete and Rome in the west, and Egypt and Arabia in the south--all chattering away in their own native languages and local dialects.

Then it happened. They heard something strange and amazing: they were hearing about the dramatic and extraordinary things God had done in and through Jesus in their own native tongues, in their own local dialects! No need for translators-- it was miraculously being done for them!

They asked, "How is this happening?" It was the Holy Spirit performing a miracle of hearing, a miracle of communication giving a group of ordinary Galileans the ability to articulate the good news of Jesus Christ in ways that could be heard and understood by people different than themselves in something as intimate and personal as their own local languages.

This miracle marked the fulfilling of God's ancient promise to bring all the nations of the world together and bless them (Gen. 12:3), but in a strange and unexpected way. Through the reconciling death of Christ on the cross and with a sudden surge of the Holy Spirit's creative power God was throwing open wide the doors of his kingdom to every Tom, Dick and Harriet, no matter who they were, where they were from or what they had done-- to those close and those far away from him! The miracle of Pentecost kicks off a work of God's Spirit in and through the Church, breaking down dividing walls and crossing over social barriers so that the whole human race would get a chance to hear the good news of God's plan to rescue and remake the world.

And how would this happen? Was God going to use angels or heavenly skywriting or telepathy? No, God would cross barriers to reach ordinary people like you and me by empowering us, the church, with his Spirit and turning us into his ambassadors.

Jesus said exactly that in his last words to his disciples before his ascension into heaven:

But you will receive power when the Holy Spirit comes upon you. And you will be my witnesses, telling people about me everywhere—in Jerusalem, throughout Judea, in Samaria, and to the ends of the earth. (Acts 1:8)

Does this mean that every follower of Jesus becomes a great preacher, evangelist or international miracle worker? Not really. The Holy Spirit makes us "witnesses" by transforming us into new creations - people in whom God's Spirit lives and expresses himself and through whom he reaches out and loves the world, and that takes as many shapes as there are people.

The Spirit continues performing the miracle of Pentecost over and over -- maybe not by duplicating the original miracle of languages but by empowering our words and actions in other creative ways. The Spirit empowers ordinary followers of Jesus all over the world, enabling them to make the message of Jesus understandable, relevant, and visible to new generations in new contexts-- speaking with their own words and lives. The Spirit enables them to live like Jesus lived and do the things he did: sharing their stories, performing acts of kindness, caring for the poor, comforting the brokenhearted, healing the sick, setting the demonized free, reaching out to the lost, the little and the least.

When I was at my lowest point in life, people very different from me, from a totally different background than mine, went out of their way and crossed a great social divide to help me. They became my kingdom ambassadors. They worked for Teen Challenge, a Christian drug program, and spoke the gospel in a language I could hear and understand-- by their actions not just their words. Although they were different than me, there was something about them that I knew I needed—they had access to power for living and for loving that attracted me and pointed me to Jesus. It was God's Spirit in them!

Pentecost means putting our lives at the disposal of the Holy Spirit and cooperating with him for the sake of others around us. This is neither natural nor easy. It's a miracle that requires our cooperation.

Pope Francis spoke of the temptation to keep the Spirit at a distance or, as he said, our tendency to "tame the Holy Spirit."

"If I may speak plainly," he said, "we want to tame the Holy Spirit because the Spirit annoys us, the Spirit moves us, pushes us - pushes the Church - to move forward, and we'd probably prefer it if the Spirit would just keep quiet and not bother us!"

How true! Pentecost is not about us having our own personal, private experiences-- speaking in tongues and becoming spiritual elitists. Pentecost shows us that, if we're being led by and filled with the Spirit, we can't ignore the world around us or keep our neighbor who is different from us at arm's length. Pentecost is about letting the Spirit bother us, annoy us, take us out of our comfort zone to actually do something-- act as Christ's ambassadors, emissaries of his love - because our comfort zone is a dead end. Pentecost is about life, love, service, community, and transformation. It's about reaching out to others so they too can "hear" and be filled and be launched into a new way of living.

The power of the Holy Spirit is given for a purpose: Christ's mission.

If you want to enjoy the power, you'll have to accept the mission.

As a community of the Spirit, we the Church, must allow the Spirit to "bother" us. Let's let him push us out of our comfort zones-- past dividing walls towards people who may be different than us but who Christ nevertheless wants to reach with his love. Let's ask the Holy Spirit to take control of our lives so he can speak the language of Christ's love through us in ways people outside our church can hear and understand and respond to. Let's put our lives at his disposal and be filled with the Spirit's presence and power.

Reflection and Action

1. What do you think are some of the "creative" ways that Mike says followers of Jesus can participate in that communicate the message of Jesus and his kingdom?

2. How do you think people and churches are guilty of trying to "tame the Holy Spirit"? What would it look like to be "naturally supernatural" as well as being radically available to follow God's guidance? How can you say "Yes" to God in the current context of your life?

3. Why do you think people often avoid reaching out to people who are different, overlooked, or marginalized? If it's connected to being uncomfortable, how does the Holy Spirit want us to deal with this?

4. Mike tells us that the power of the Holy Spirit is given for the purpose of Christ's mission. If we want more of the Holy Spirit's work in our lives, we need to accept Jesus' mission. How would you describe God's mission and where can you get involved in it right now?

14 SHAKE, RATTLE & ROLL

Some people seem more prone to spiritual experiences than others, but, as a pastor acquaintance of mine put it, "we're all mystically wired." Created in God's image, we humans have a capacity and a hunger for relationship with him, but ever since things went terribly wrong in the garden (Gen 2:4-3:24), experiencing God is harder to come by and less straightforward. Nowadays there's much confusion and controversy surrounding spiritual experiences. We crave them, but at the same time they also trouble and frighten us because they're often strange and weird.

Nevertheless, there are a number of Christians who are fascinated with spiritual experiences and obsessed with "manifestations." They want them badly. They crave tongues and prophecy, to be slain in the Spirit or have a vision, to have God speak in a dream... Oh, to be visited by an angel or feel the power of God shake, rattle and roll through their bodies!

I'm being facetious, of course. But the danger is that, while these experiences are real and can be extremely valuable, they're largely misunderstood and mishandled. One of the most common mistakes is to attach a false sense of importance and validation to oneself as the result of a spiritual experience. It's easy to conclude that an experience like giving a prophetic message or receiving a vision is a sign of one's spiritual superiority or God's approval and endorsement of one's life. It is neither. That kind of thinking is a misunderstanding of grace.

I've experienced plenty-- far more than I can explain. I've ridden the Third Wave. I've soaked in the Toronto Blessing.

I've hung out with mystics like Lonnie Frisbee. And I've had a myriad of less spectacular experiences in between. Still, my grasp of these things-- as well as my ability to explain them-- is limited. I merely share as a participant, an interested observer, and as a pastor.

The power is actually a person with a purpose

Let's start with the Holy Spirit himself. The Spirit is referred to as a "he" not an "it." (John 14:26; 16:14). He's a divine person, not an impersonal power like the Force in Star Wars. The Holy Spirit is a person in the same sense that the Father is a person and the Son is a person. As a person, he can be known. We can develop a relationship with him in the same way as with the Father and Jesus. We can enjoy intimate fellowship with him and commune with him.

So when we experience the Holy Spirit, we're experiencing God. And when we experience God, it's not random, pointless, or frivolous. God isn't in the entertainment business or keen on giving us the warm fuzzies. When we experience the Holy Spirit, he's *doing* something. He has a purpose in mind that always has something to do with our role in his kingdom.

On the Day of Pentecost the Spirit didn't pour himself out on those hundred and twenty disciples in the upper room just to rock their world and give them a great story to share with their grandkids someday. The Spirit was equipping them to carry on Christ's mission (Acts 1:8). When Saul ran into Christ on the road to Damascus, he wasn't being taught a lesson for all the trouble he had been causing the Church. God was drafting Saul into his service. And later when Paul was filled with the Spirit and received back his sight when Ananias laid hands on him, it wasn't so he could return to business as usual. He was being given power and authority to bring the gospel to the Gentile world (Acts 9:15-19).

I've noticed that when the Spirit shows up, whether dramatically or subtlety, it's consistently to do one of three things: bring people *closer* to himself, *heal* them in some way, or *empower* them for service-- and occasionally some combination of all three simultaneously.

Experiences

By *spiritual experiences* I mean encountering God in some way and by *manifestations* I'm referring to our (often physical) responses when we experience God. They go hand in hand. Let's take a look first at experiences.

People experience God in varying ways. We don'tt all experience the Spirit the same way. It's not one size fits all. It depends on a lot of things, such as what's been taught, models we've seen, expectations and how a person is "wired." Some people are emotional or intuitive so their experience of God can be visceral and emotional. It can get physical: they "feel" God. Others are wired artistically. If they're visually inclined, they may experience God by means of images, visions and other visual "promptings." Others are more stoic and unemotional. They experience God, but you couldn't tell by the looks of it.

I've been in gatherings when the Spirit began to move around the room and people reacted in lots of different ways simultaneously: one person is crying, while the person next to her is laughing, and the person behind her is shaking. Across the aisle, someone is sitting peacefully with the Lord, oblivious of the guy in the next seat who just passed out! The way we experience God is individual.

Manifestations

On the whole, most Christians are open to spiritual experiences, at least to a degree. The Bible gives us a grid for the supernatural: the idea that God can speak to us out of the blue isn't such a stretch. A God that whispers to his children is within the realm of possibility and reason. The same goes for the idea of God placing a sense of burden on our hearts. It doesn't upset or confuse us. We can understand why God might talk to us or give us a concern or some sense of urgency. But what about the stranger spiritual phenomena? Why would God make someone "drunk" or make them laugh or cry hysterically? Why would God cause someone to jerk and spazz-out like they have palsy? It's crazy. It's disruptive, it offends our minds, and it's embarrassing and weird. What good could possibly come of it? These kind of questions lead some to conclude that such things can't be from God!

John Wimber wrote: *Neither I nor the Bible equate phenomena such as falling, shaking, crying out, laughing or making animal noises with an experience with God. However you may have an experience with God that may result in some of those responses... [These kinds of phenomena are] not necessarily anything that we ought to equate as "always" something of God, or even "sometimes" something of God, thought [they] may be a reaction to the Spirit's activity. (Vineyard Reflections: Refreshing, Renewal, and Revival; Vol. 2 Issue 4; July/August 1994)*

The Bible doesn't answer these questions about the meaning or purpose of such manifestations; it just attests to them.

It simply takes for granted that they occur. We can only offer our best guesses based on the witness of the Scripture and experience. So allow me to offer mine:

The most helpful explanation of these sorts of phenomena came from Wimber. He used an illustration from the field of meteorology. Do you know what happens when a mass of cold air and a mass of warm air run into each other? They create instability in the atmosphere, and you get a thunderstorm. Sometimes this interaction is especially violent and produces tornadoes. When two forces collide, it's called a "power encounter," and, like a thunderstorm, it can be explosive and messy. What happens in nature with the weather happens in the spiritual realm in the encounter between God's kingdom and the kingdom of Satan and the kingdom of Self (Matthew 12:22-29). When those kingdoms collide, there is a power encounter and, instead of thunderstorms and tornadoes, there's shaking and quaking and other strange physical and emotional phenomena that also can be explosive and messy as a result of the clash.

In the gospel accounts, the mere presence of Jesus threw demonized people into a frenzy. There was always an enormous commotion as they yelled and pleaded with him to leave them alone. When the mob came to arrest Jesus in the garden, they were thrown backward to the ground as Jesus stepped forward and identified himself, the result of a power encounter between God's Spirit in Jesus and his kingdom and the power of hatred and violence in them (John 18:6).

In my opinion, many of the manifestations that occur in God's presence are a reflection of this sort of power encounter. I've seen them when praying for the sick and the healing power of the Spirit confronts the power of a life-threatening illness or serious injury head-on. The encounter is often accompanied by strong physical phenomena like heat, shaking or falling down (what some refer to as "being slain in the Spirit." When a longstanding, destructive emotional wound in a person's soul is overwhelmed by the healing presence of God's love during worship. there can be a forceful, sometimes bizarre reaction. And when a demonic stronghold in a person's is invaded by the liberating power of God's Spirit, it's usually not without a messy struggle — a power encounter.

Again, Wimber commented on this: *We've seen various vocal expressions of roaring, moaning, crying out or screaming. We've also seen an increase in what we might call the emotional responses: laughing, crying, screaming.*

Whereas many Bible characters responded emotionally to God from time to time, I don't see any place where the Scripture endorses or recommends that activity, other than it might relate to repentance. These are just some of the varied ways human beings respond to an encounter with God, so therefore they can be allowed. (Vineyard Reflections: Refreshing, Renewal And Revival, Vol. 2 Issue 4, July/August 1994)

Not everything that looks to be psychotic or demonic or even like human enthusiasm may be what it appears. One person may have a genuine response to the presence of the Spirit which involves shaking or falling down. A person standing next to him or her may do the same exact thing out of emotionalism or some other excess. Therefore, we shouldn't rush to judgment. Prayerful caution and biblical discernment are needed.

Our human explanations of spiritual experiences often fall short. Not every experience can be explained. Some things are a mystery because there's much about God we don't understand. But one thing is for sure: the test of any experience should be whether or not it directs our attention to Christ. When all is said and done, do I love Jesus more? Do I trust him more? Am I committed to serving him more? The important thing is whether or not, in the aftermath of my experience I'm walking closer to God.

The bottom line
I know this is going to sound strange with all the attention given to spiritual experiences and manifestations, but they're no big deal really. They're incidental to the real, meaningful work of the Spirit. Like king Saul, a person can have a powerful experience with no lasting effect on his or her life (1Sam. 10:9-11). They can shake, rattle, roll and prophesy meeting after meeting with no lasting evidence of godly transformation and discipleship whatsoever. In that case, all they had was an experience. Conversely, a person can be deeply moved and radically changed by God while not exhibiting any visible sign at all.

The bottom line in spiritual experiences and manifestations should be changed lives. What really matters is the fruit that they bear. Wimber would say, "I don't care how a tree shakes, it's the fruit that counts." What really matters are people transformed into empowered and compassionate servants by the power of God. Experiences and manifestations go with the territory. But they're incidental. They should be allowed to happen without endorsing, encouraging or stimulating them as if they were ends in themselves. We should be moved by the Spirit away from a "bless me" kind of focus to a "bless others" focus.

In other words, as exciting, even intoxicating, it may be when God shows up and strange things begin to happen, experiences and manifestations shouldn't become our focus. Jesus and his kingdom should be. It shouldn't be about "having an experience." It should be about surrendering and making ourselves available to the King and directing the blessings that come as a result of experiencing the Spirit into activities that will minister and bless those outside the walls of our churches. It should translate into things like loving one another and our neighbors and caring for the poor, the weak, the broken, and the lost.

Reflection and Action

1. Many polls have revealed that while people are becoming less *religious,* they are still very *spiritual.* In fact, many people have unexplainable spiritual experiences. How might this be an opportunity for the church to carry out Jesus' mission?

2. Have you ever had a spiritual experience? How did this enhance (or distract) from your relationship with Jesus? What was the fruit from that experience?

3. As Mike teaches us that the "power is a person," how can we grow in our relationship with the Holy Spirit? What practices and habits will strengthen our connection and ability to follow his lead?

4. In order to discern truth in the midst of "manifestations," what fruit (evidence) should accompany any activity of the Holy Spirit?

5. What would it look like to be grounded in love and humility as a community experiences the power and presence of God in a way that causes or allows for spiritual experiences and certain manifestations? How could this help with church unity and enhance discipleship?

6. Mike seems to warn against making manifestations a central focus of our gatherings (as well as our individual lives). What should our focus be? What will help to keep a healthy focus?

15 EXPANDING OUR UNDERSTANDING AND EXPECTATIONS FOR THE SPIRIT'S WORK

BY LUKE GERATY

One of my favorite theologians, Jürgen Moltmann, says that "The gift and the presence of the Holy Spirit is the greatest and most wonderful thing which we can experience." My own experiences have confirmed this to be true and reading *I'm No Superman* only verified my commitment to be a follower of Jesus who deeply values the empowering presence of the Holy Spirit in my own life and the lives of those whom I am in community with.

I actually grew up in "charismatic" churches, with the bulk of my time spent in the Vineyard. These types of churches are definitely "home" for me, and I've learned so much about the kingdom of God while being around them. I've learned how to pray for the sick, how to hear from God, how to respond to what I sense the Holy Spirit doing, and so much more! My appreciation for the Charismatic Tradition goes deep.

But I also love the whole Church and believe that the Holy Spirit has been at work in other parts of the Church and as I've studied church history and theology, I've only become more convinced that John Wimber was correct when he suggested the Church was a stew with lots of different vegetables and flavors. In the words of the Apostle Paul, "our knowledge is partial and incomplete" (1 Cor. 13:9). We need each other and can learn from how the Holy Spirit has worked throughout church history as well as in other Christian traditions.

Exploring Spaces *of* the Spirit

I've found that many "charismatics" tend to see the activity of the Spirit as primarily encompassing supernatural ministry. Much of the focus is upon spiritual gifts such as prophecy, healing, demonic deliverance, and speaking in tongues. Obviously, this isn't *all* that the Holy Spirit does, but if we're honest and self-aware, this is what tends to receive most of the emphasis in our corner of the Church.

When I began studying theology, I began to discover that other traditions actually saw the work of the Spirit in *other* areas of Christian life. Some emphasized the work of the Spirit in the process of salvation. Others understood the Holy Spirit as being deeply concerned with issues of social justice and was calling the church to advocate against slavery, for ethnic reconciliation, and for human flourishing. Some of my more liturgical leaning sisters and brothers in Christ spent a great deal of time directing their attention to the Spirit's work in the Sacraments (or Ordinances).

What if the Holy Spirit is involved in a lot more than we realize? How could the Church become more *responsive* if it were more *aware* of where the Spirit was working?

I think we actually need to "thicken" our theology of the Holy Spirit! From start to finish, the Holy Spirit is *everywhere* in Scripture. For example, in Genesis 1:2 we read that the Holy Spirit was present at Creation. In the last chapter of Revelation, we read that the Spirit invites and urges people to come to Jesus.

It appears rather safe to acknowledge that there are many spaces of the Spirit.

Creating Spaces *for* the Spirit

As I've concluded that the Spirit's working far more than I could possibly imagine, I've begun asking questions about how I could be more intentional at creating spaces *for* the Spirit to work. While Mike did a wonderful job in his chapter on "Midwifing" in relation to how you can help people receive ministry from the Holy Spirit, what about the spaces that exist in our worship gatherings or Christian life where the Spirit also works?

For example, how does the Holy Spirit work in the following contexts:

- Baptism?
- Communion?
- Discipleship?
- Preaching?
- Worship?
- Marriage?
- Parenting?
- Singleness?

These are just a few of the areas where I believe we need to expand our understanding of the Holy Spirit's work. If we really think about it, *the sky is the limit for how and where the Holy Spirit works!*

This is why millions of Christians all over the world regularly pray an invitation for the Holy Spirit to empower *every* area of their life. And this is why many "charismatic" churches now tie the work of the Spirit to one's baptism and regularly celebrate Communion as a space for the Holy Spirit to engage people's hearts and minds.

As an example of this enlarged understanding and appreciation of the Spirit's work here's a suggestion on how churches can expand and thicken their celebration of the Lord's Supper as a space for the Holy Spirit's activity.

Spirit and Supper

In the early church, the Lord's Supper was a central aspect of worship. It was a regular rhythm for followers of Jesus to *remember* his death on the Cross. Celebrating Communion caused the Church to *re-center* on the sacrificial nature of God's kingdom while also *renewing* disciples with the radical love displayed in Jesus' crucifixion. While we know *what* was being remembered (Jesus' death), I think we need to better understand *who* is at work re-centering and renewing the Church – the Holy Spirit!

As the Church gathers to worship and comes to the Lord's Table, they receive the Bread and Cup as a step toward experiencing God's presence. And as any good Bible student knows, God's presence is experienced by the Holy Spirit. The Spirit was poured out on the Church (Acts 2; Romans 8) and gives life, empowers for ministry, sanctifies, and mediates God's love to the Church. Put bluntly, we experience God because and when we experience the Spirit.

Any encounter with God that we have takes place because we have come in contact with God's Spirit!

One theologian suggested that when we receive Communion, the Holy Spirit's presence actually helps us "feast" on the Risen and Ascended Christ. This is why I believe that when we faithfully celebrate the Lord's Supper, we are creating a space for the Spirit to work – and work the Spirit does!

Several years ago, our church was celebrating Communion together and what happened next could *only* be described as an "outpouring" of the Holy Spirit. While we were, together, remembering the broken Body and shed blood of Christ, numerous people began to, for the first time, experience the tremendous love of God. Others came under conviction for things they had done that had hurt their relationship with God and others. Still more began to step forward to minister to others with words of prophecy and prayers for healing. People were set free, empowered, healed, and received words of comfort, strength, and encouragement.

It was incredible.

And guess what? The relationship between Communion and the Spirit is found *right in the Bible!* If you take a look at 1 Corinthians, you'll notice that the Apostle Paul teaches on the Lord's Supper in 1 Cor. 11:17-34 and then launches into a discussion of the spiritual gifts in chapters 12-14. For the Apostle Paul, there was no separation from discussing the work of the Spirit in relation to Communion and the work of the Spirit with spiritual gifts. In fact, it was a natural progression in his thought.

Conclusion
As we "charismatics" continue to emphasize the Holy Spirit beyond the margins of Christian life, let us consider remembering that when Jesus promised to build his Church (Matthew 16:18), he meant it. And the way in which Jesus is building his Church is through the presence and power of the Spirit. The richer our theology of the Spirit is, the more our practices are enhanced. For God theology *always* enriches the Church.

Thus, when we say, "Come Holy Spirit," let us invite and anticipate the Spirit's work in everything and everywhere. May the Spirit come in power in both our singing and our praying, in our homes and in our places of vocation. May we expect the Spirit's activity when we gather to receive Communion or when we engage in the process of discipleship.

As Moltmann has also described the Holy Spirit as giving the Church "vitalizing energy," my prayer is that we would be energized to carry out "Holy Spirit ministry" for the glory of God and the well-being of people.

Reflection and Action

1. Luke cautions having too narrow of a view of the Holy Spirit's work. Why might limiting the Spirit's activity to signs and wonders be limiting to one's awareness, responsiveness and experiencing the abundant life Jesus promised?

2. In what way(s) does Luke's statement: "Thus, when we say, 'Come Holy Spirit,' let us invite and anticipate the Spirit's work in everything and everywhere", line up Paul's exhortation, *"And whatever you do, whether in word or deed, do it all in the name of the Lord Jesus, giving thanks to God the Father through him." (Col. 3:17)*

3. "...The Spirit is at work all over the place in our lives, in the work of the Church, and in the world around us." What practices and habits can we develop that will heighten our awareness of the Spirit in this way?

4. How would more awareness of the presence and leading of the Holy Spirit enhance your participation in the Lord's Supper and water baptism?

5. How can you become more intentional about creating spaces *for* the Spirit to work in other areas and everyday activities of your life such as at work and school? What practices and habits can you develop that will heighten your awareness of the Spirit's presence and work in the ordinary?

16 RACHAEL'S STORY

I'm no superman, but there have been times - every once in a blue moon - where God has allowed me passage into what is, for me, the rarified territory of the truly miraculous. I'm not a native in that land: I'm an immigrant who is barely able to speak the language. But my occasional visits are enough to convince me that God is still in the business of performing mind-blowing miracles today and that, if we dare to pay attention and make ourselves available to him, we can get in on these uncommon, unparalleled, and breathtaking moments.

I'd like to close with one such miracle story I had the good fortune to be part of. It's the story of Rachael, a young lady I met in 2005 at a Vineyard conference in the Poconos.

Rachael had just completed a Master's degree in opera and was looking for work. She heard that Arizona Opera was holding auditions for their outreach tour, so she bought a plane ticket and auditioned for the staff there. They notified her before the day was over that they wanted to offer her a contract. She returned to Philadelphia in the knowledge that she was finally a gainfully employed singer and that she had two weeks to pack up her belongings and head to Arizona for four months. Once she got there and started performing, she realized that being on tour was not as glamorous as it sounded. The company traveled by van, slept in a different hotel room every night, and loaded and unloaded their own sets. After just two weeks, Rachael's hip started bothering her. She had a pain in her side and a knot in her back.

After a few weeks of yoga and lots of aspirin with no relief, Rachael decided to go to an urgent care unit.

They blamed stress and prescribed some narcotics. But the narcotics didn't make the pain in her side go away, and the knot in her back seemed to actually grow worse. One particular day, the pain in her back and side got so bad that she asked one of the other singers to take her to the emergency room. The doctors there couldn't find any evidence of why she was in pain, again blamed stress, prescribed some stronger narcotics, and sent her on my way.

When those stronger narcotics failed to relieve Rachael's pain, she knew she was in trouble. She decided that she needed to take a break from the tour and get to a doctor who could actually diagnose the source of all her pain. She flew to Florida, where her mom was, to get some tests done that would hopefully lead to a cure for her aching body. After a couple of weeks and still with no explanation for her pain besides stress, Rachael started feeling like her legs were asleep. The tingly feeling didn't go away and after a couple of days she started to lose feeling in her legs altogether. Her mom took her to the emergency room, where they immediately ordered an M.R.I. As soon as the test was over, the neurologist delivered the news that Rachael had a large tumor on her spine and that it was probably cancer. Rachael and her mom were shocked. She had otherwise been healthy-- this was the last thing she expected to hear at twenty-four years old.

Rachael spent the next few weeks getting biopsies and all sorts of scans. The doctors ordered radiation and a strong dose of steroids to reduce the size of the tumor and the amount of pressure it was putting on her spine. They hoped that by doing this she might someday be able to walk again. After several weeks of waiting, her oncologist had an official diagnosis: Rachael had aggressive, stage 4 non-Hodgkin's Lymphoma (a blood cancer that most commonly affects men in their sixties and later). There was evidence that the cancer had spread throughout her entire body and therefore needed to be treated right away-- with eight rounds of chemotherapy. The nurse explained to her that chemo would last five months and that Rachael would need to have surgery in order for a port to be placed in her chest to receive her treatments. She would definitely lose her hair.

Within a month of starting treatments, she was totally bald. The chemo made her nauseous at some times and hungry at others. She still hadn't regained the ability to walk on her own, so she had to use a walker around the house and had to be in a wheelchair when she went out. Rachael's mom took a leave of absence from her job-- doing physical therapy with kids-- to take care of her. It was not easy at all. Rachael was twenty-four years old, and there she was having her mom do everything for her.

She had all these dreams for her life: dreams of singing all over the world with Philadelphia as her home base, dreams of financial independence... and there she was in Florida with all of those dreams crushed. She would be lucky just to walk on her own again. It was devastating.

During the first two months of treatment, Rachael's focus was on relearning to walk and figuring out how to deal with the side effects of chemo. As she tells it, she didn't take much time to focus on her soul. She found herself feeling more and more depressed and angry. Her doctor offered to put her on anti-depressants. While she thought that they could be really helpful, she also knew that she would have to stay on them for a while even after the cancer was gone, and she didn't want to be dependent on them. So she decided to try going to church before committing to yet another prescription.

The miracle begins

Growing up, Rachael's family didn't even have a Bible, let alone attend church, so she looked online to find a church in her hometown of St. Petersburg. As it turned out, there was a fairly new Vineyard church plant in town, and she asked her mom to drive her there the following Sunday. Even though her mom wasn't into the whole Jesus thing, she knew how important it was to her daughter so she agreed to drive her but didn't go in. After Rachael went the first few weeks by herself and gave her stamp of approval, her mom decided to come inside with her instead of dropping her off. They both found the people there to be extremely friendly and very faithful, and, with the help of this loving St. Pete Vineyard family, God healed Rachael of her depression.

As the months of chemo went on, Rachael's test results came back showing some improvement. She expected that, once she had completed all eight rounds of chemo, the tests would come back completely clear, with no evidence of cancer. But that's not what happened. Rachael had scans done right after she finished treatment, two weeks later, and then six weeks later, and they all showed "activity," which could have been either cancer or residual effects from the chemo. Whatever it was, it didn't matter to Rachael: her doctors couldn't tell her that the cancer was gone. She had completed a process that she thought would cure her, but it seemed that God was taking his time in bringing healing. She would have to accept what her doctors said – she might always have pain in her back, and she might never walk normally again, despite the five months of treatment she had just undergone.

A surprise in the Poconos

Rachael found out that our Vineyard Eastern Regional Conference would be happening in the Poconos that July and that some of her friends from the West Philly Vineyard would be going. Since she had just finished chemo and didn't have anything else going on, she booked her plane ticket to go to Pennsylvania to go to the conference.

Here's how she described what happened next: "The conference was great. The worship was really powerful, and the teachings were excellent, but, to me, the most wonderful thing about that week was a workshop that Mike Turrigiano from the North Brooklyn Vineyard led, called *Midwifing the Holy Spirit*. I went to the workshop wanting to learn how to better pray for others and hoping to see the Holy Spirit do some cool stuff. I don't think I believed that God could want to do the cool stuff to <u>me</u>. After all, I had already been through eight rounds of chemo, and I had been prayed for lots of times by lots of different people. It seemed to me that God must not have wanted to do a miraculous healing for me in the moment, and I was sure that my healing would be a more gradual one.

"Once Mike went over how to 'bless what the Father is doing,' he told us that we were going to do just that. We would pray as a group and, as we were doing that, he would be watching to see if God was up to anything. He pulled a few people out of the circle into the middle of the room and asked the people around them to pray for them...he [continued to] ma[ke] his way around the room looking for what God wanted to do. He called me into the middle and started [by] simply praying for healing. But then he started praying for the exact things that only God and I had talked about, things that I hadn't told anyone else. I left that workshop feeling like I had actually been in God's presence and thinking about how cool it was that God used this stranger from New York to speak directly to me. I wasn't convinced that He had actually healed me, but it was nice to know that God was there and that He had been listening to my prayers. I also appreciated that someone new was reminding God that I was still there, in pain, and waiting for His slow healing process to be complete.

"That night there was a party at Mike's villa, and our west Philly group went to meet new people and connect with old friends. While we were there, I told our pastor Becca about what happened in the workshop and how Mike had been right on with everything he was praying. She asked me if I told him that he was onto something. I guess it would have been a logical thing to do, but, no, I hadn't.

She encouraged me to find him right away and let him know that he really was hearing from God and that every word from his mouth seemed like it was from the Holy Spirit. It didn't quite seem like the most comfortable thing to do, but I knew Becca wasn't going to let me get away with not doing it."

Let me butt into Rachael's story: When I first saw Rachael in the workshop, even though she still had a crew cut and was quite pale and frail looking, cancer hadn't crossed my mind. Later, when she showed up at our party with her friends, there was a group of us sitting outside just hanging out-- old friends catching up, drinking beer, smoking cigars, and shooting the breeze. Nothing more. Ministry was the furthest thing from my mind. So what happened next was totally unexpected...

"Mike was outside with some other Vineyard leaders enjoying his party and relaxing. I quietly interrupted the conversation and told Mike how powerful the prayer in his workshop had really been..."

As Rachael shared her story with us, the mood changed, and things got serious. My heart broke for her as she told the story of her ordeal. Right there in the middle of our party, I began sensing the presence of the Spirit hovering over us. I could tell by the expressions on everyone's faces that they did too. I knew what he was asking us to do...

Rachael continues:
"Mike asked a few questions about my treatment and how I was feeling, and then all of the guys put down their cigars to lay hands on me and pray for God to heal me-- right there, in the middle of the party! It was so cool to feel so cared for and valued. There was no bolt of lightning to tell me that God healed me, but I walked away feeling good about the prayer time."

We prayed, but, honestly, there was no indication that anything dramatic had happened. So, as quickly as the mood had grown serious, after we finished praying, it shifted back, and we continued partying...

Little did we know that something had happened. I'll let Rachael explain:

"The next day, during worship, I felt different. For the first time in my life, I felt completely free to worship God in a way that I had never felt free to worship before. I also started feeling a tingling in my back: right where the primary tumor had been, and where the doctor said I would always have pain, I felt a tingling sensation.

It was in that moment that I knew God had actually finally brought healing."

Rachael went back home to her mom in Florida and shared what had happened. Her mother was starting to really like what she saw God doing in Rachael's life, and this was just further proof that there might be something more to faith in Jesus. But they both still needed hard evidence from the doctors that Rachael was healed.

Her next scan was scheduled for a month later. Rachael spent the month leading up to it getting ready to move back to Philly. She knew that was where God was calling her, and she knew that he was going to provide a way for her to get back there. She even set a goal date and started preparing to move on September 1, 2006. Rachael went in for her scan, waited for the results, and found out on September 7 that she was officially in remission. There was no longer any evidence of cancer in her body! She got on a plane two days later to move back to Philly. Her health has been great ever since!

Ripple effect
Rachael moved back in Philadelphia where she has seen God surpass her expectations. The dreams that she held onto so tightly before cancer changed. Touring the world singing didn't quite look like she thought it would. Instead, she got a full-time job in education and began singing for the joy of singing and worshiping God and has had some amazing opportunities to share what God has done in her life. She still enjoys making music, but now as a form of worship rather than as a way to make a living.

As Rachael explains:

"The most amazing thing that has happened since my healing has been seeing my mom come to know Jesus and trust Him with her life. She jokes that she's sorry it took me getting cancer for her to understand just how incredible God is. I know that wasn't the reason I got sick. I know that God could have gotten through to her in other ways. God didn't make me sick or want me to be sick. The fact that we live in a broken world is the reason that I got sick. And my healing was just one example of His kingdom breaking into this fallen world. God used that horrible experience to make himself known. It is one of my new dreams that He will continue to use my sickness to encourage others and to bring some hope into this world that can seem hopeless at times."

Rachael is now a dear friend of mine and my wife's.

She's a person who radiates joy whenever we're together. Today she's happily married and serves as a chaplain at Main Line Hospice providing spiritual and emotional support to hospice patients and their loved ones. She's a testimony of the Lord's amazing, mind-blowing love and miraculous power. Her story is an example of how we are invited to partner with the in-the-moment ministry of the Holy Spirit – those unexpected, unplanned instances when the kingdom of God breaks in on us and heaven touches earth to bring healing and new life. I believe God can use every one of us in these naturally supernatural ways. Because most Christians lack training in how to be alert and respond in these moments, we miss tremendous opportunities to help people and to make Jesus Christ famous.

Get in on the action
Maybe this is all strange and new to you. Perhaps you never heard before you read this book about praying for the sick or healing before. It sounds like something straight out of a Harry Potter novel with magic and flying broomsticks. Or maybe you've disqualified yourself by thinking that God only uses the prayers of spiritual superstars. Actually, there is no such thing as a spiritual superstar-- only ordinary people like you and me, who love Jesus, listen to his Spirit, and are willing to be child-like enough to trust and obey what he tells us to do.

I'm not saying we're all meant to be full-time miracle workers. But I believe that each one of us can develop the basic know-how necessary to pray for someone with sensitivity and confidence if the need should arise. Imagine Jesus using you to help someone like Rachael who needs a healing touch... a miracle. I don't think this is a stretch at all: I believe he wants to. But it won't happen magically. First, you have to make yourself *available*. Then the Lord will make you *able* by his Spirit.

Reflection and Action

1. As you read Rachael's story, what stood out to you?

2. Why are stories like this so important to share? Do you have a story of a miracle that you can share?

3. Before Mike prayed for Rachael the second time, he sensed the Spirit hovering over them. What does this mean? Since everyone can learn how to sense this, how can you learn to recognize when this happens?

4. Rachael's healing seemed to be a process requiring more than one prayer. What does this tell you about the work of the Spirit and the nature of miracles?

5. If God is still in the business of doing miracles, how are you going to step into a position where you can see them happen more often? What needs to change in your life immediately? Who can you pray for now?

APPENDIX: THE OFT OVERLOOKED INGREDIENT IN CHURCH PLANTING

At the risk of being too simple, I'd say successful church planting boils down to being the right person in the right place following God's Spirit at the right time. Yet, surprisingly, the essential dimension of the power and guidance of the Holy Spirit is often overlooked in church planting strategy. Francis Schaeffer once commented: "The central problem of our age is the church of the Lord Jesus Christ, individually or corporately, tending to do the Lord's work in the power of the flesh rather than of the Spirit."

Too often church planting is carried out with a mindset that omits the supernatural. A lot of church planters are poorly informed about the supernatural mechanics of the Holy Spirit: they're either unfamiliar with him or untutored in the art of listening to him. The Book of Acts—the original church planting narrative, you might say-- makes a big deal of the Spirit's regularly speaking and guiding Jesus's earliest followers by means of angels, visions, dreams, and other supernatural operations. He's revealed as the Spirit of missions, the main ingredient in church planting, giving birth to the Church at Pentecost and heading up the church planting business from the beginning.

Our basic operating procedure: doing what the Father is doing

It might seem obvious that the best way to carry on Christ's ministry would be to adopt Christ's methods. "…as the Father has sent me I am sending you". Unfortunately, most Western Christians would rather implement methods and programs that reduce ministry to reproducible components to be applied indiscriminately than operate the way Jesus did. Now, there's nothing wrong with developing and utilizing tools for team building or evangelism or launching public services, but should they be used arbitrarily-- or all the time in every instance? I don't think so.

Shouldn't we first ask what's appropriate for each situation and discern what God is doing, the way Jesus did?

Jesus did all the things necessary for a vibrant, worldwide church planting movement by paying close attention to his Father. How? Well, we're told that he "often went off to be by himself and pray." He evidently found time to un-busy himself, get alone with his Father, and pray-- making it possible for him to keep in step with the Holy Spirit and do what the Father was doing.

I think Jesus used whatever approach his Father directed him to use in each particular situation as it presented itself. It appears that his powerful "naturally supernatural" public ministry was the result of his cultivating the inner conditions of his soul that enabled him to pay attention, listen, and obey the promptings of his Father. This might give us a clue as to why he would go out of his way to address the despised Zacchaeus sitting up in a tree, or heal just that one man at the pool, when apparently there were many sick people waiting and hoping to be healed. Listening to the Father by the Spirit seemed to be his standard operating procedure for doing kingdom work and the pattern he left for us to follow (John 5:19, 30).

That's why in the Vineyard we try to enter each ministry situation with the question, "What's the Father doing?" With this as our rule of thumb, making the decisions and exercising the spiritual gifts necessary for planting a church becomes a matter of discerning what the Father is up to and then joining in with the help of the Holy Spirit.

Paying attention and listening become essential skills because Jesus is the project manager of every church plant. It is, after all, his ministry. His authority, not ours, gets the job done. Our part is to cooperate and get on with his agenda. It's the Lord who conceives, gives birth to, builds, and adds to the church, not us--no matter how dedicated, smart, and gifted we are. He graciously stoops to use our efforts. Church planting philosophy and practices, though helpful, only tell us where to seed, water, and prune and what fertilizer to use. In no way do they cause or even explain the miracle of the birth and growth of the Body of Christ (1 Cor 3:6-7). That's God's business.

I think that the Vineyard's extraordinary early success in church planting was due to the empowering of the Spirit rather than our strategy, training, or planning. To be honest, many of us were underprepared and in over our heads but succeeded nonetheless. Having our imaginations captured by a fresh vision of the kingdom of God and our lives set on fire by the power of the Holy Spirit (more than) made up for what we lacked in training, resources, and experience. And let's not forget how *power evangelism* played into this success. In addition to sharing their stories and inviting just about everyone they met to join in their venture, Vineyard church planters regularly prayed for the sick and casually shared prophetic words as well as words of knowledge that opened the eyes and hearts of even hardened skeptics to the presence, love, and power of God, increasing their receptivity and the odds that they'd show up to church and begin following Jesus.

I'm not saying that training, tools, and planning are not important--even necessary. They absolutely are! But relying heavily on methods and systems rather than the Spirit is putting the cart before the horse. We need the Holy Spirit's presence and power in church planting. He's our main ingredient.

No Spirit, no Church

The Spirit launched the first disciples into the church planting business. Without the Spirit there are no church planters or churches. He makes the church the Church. Is it possible to successfully plant a church without the power of the Holy Spirit? You can argue that a group of talented, charismatic leaders can draw a crowd and form it into a community. You can find the right creative team, talented musicians, and speakers, attract a lot of people, and call it a "church". But it doesn't mean you have a church. A growing and energetic assembly is not necessarily evidence of the Holy Spirit's work. Every week there are plenty of growing and lively gatherings that are not. Thousands of Mormons, Muslims, Unitarians, Jehovah's Witness, Christian Scientists, and Scientologists gather each week for worship. There are hundreds of dead "Christian" churches that gather weekly that deny the gospel. In other words, it's possible to successfully plant a community without the power of the Holy Spirit and call it a church. But it won't be a church – a community of the Holy Spirit (1 Cor 3:16).

Spirit-driven Church Planting

It should go without saying, then, that a church planter should be Spirit-filled. But what does that mean? It centers on the issue of control. The word "filled" that Paul uses in Ephesians 5:18 carries the idea of living "constantly under the control of..." In other words, being filled by the Spirit doesn't mean we get more of him: he gets more of us-- more trust, more access to us, more cooperation from us. It's almost the opposite of relying on training muscle, smarts, and sheer dedication to succeed. The Spirit-filled life is a life of surrender and dependency. At times, it's more about *not doing* than doing. It's about learning to abide and exercising *quiet acceptance* (something Jesus himself was really good at). It's about trusting, paying attention, and following the promptings of the Spirit so that you can stay in step with him and the Father. And all of this is activated and worked out through listening prayer, the way it was in Jesus' life.

The good news is that the Holy Spirit is just as ready to shape, empower, and guide church planting today as he was back in Ephesus and Corinth. The Holy Spirit is an expert church planter, but he hasn't reduced church planting into a broadly reproducible model. He's tied it to a dependent relationship.

My best advice to church planters is to develop an ever-deepening, intimate, dependent relationship with the Holy Spirit and make it your aim to keep in step with him.

Each church plant is distinct and special. God is busy at work in a unique way in each location and situation. Each presents a unique challenge of discerning what the Father's up to and joining in. The Holy Spirit's power and guidance is essential, and he's ready to lead every step of the way. He's the expert so we don't have to be. But planters have to trust, pray, stay alert, keep in step with him, and work hard nevertheless. Above all, this means they'll have to constantly choose between the Spirit's leadership and their own.

Made in the USA
Middletown, DE
22 July 2019